Rhythmic Activities and Dance

John Price Bennett, EdD
University of North Carolina at Wilmington

Pamela Coughenour Riemer, BS
Sycamore Lane Middle School
Laurinburg, North Carolina

Human Kinetics

John Price Bennett dedicates this book to:

Lenoah Long Bennett, my mother and first dance partner,
Claudia Adams Bennett, my wife and lifelong dance partner,
Zachariah Price Bennett and Rebecca Adams Bennett, my children,
and Gladys Andrews Fleming, my mentor and life-changing dance teacher.

Pamela Coughenour Riemer dedicates this book to:

Carri Riemer, my wonderful daughter, who gave me the inspiration to enhance the lives of all children by showing her eagerness and enthusiasm by dancing for life's high,

Nellie Briles Coughenour and Charlie Pearson Coughenour, my parents who encouraged me and allowed me to be me,

Sandra Coughenour Chandler and Sallie Coughenour Crossley, my sisters, who truly believed my dreams were possible,

Charlie Pearson Coughenour, Jr., "Peary," my brother, who understands my drive and creativity,

William Alfred Riemer, "Bill," my husband, who wants me to be me most of the time and gives me the time and space I need.

My friends who were instrumental in guiding me:

Eric Brooks DeGroat, my colossal mentor,
Dr. Sidney and Wilma Andrews, my wonderful friends,
Nick Nicholson, my adventure buddy,
Mary Kay Ollis, who listened and loved,
Jane McCorkle, a superior coach,
Beverly Patton, a supporting friend indeed,
Appalachian State University,
Sycamore Lane Dance Company,
and *all* of my students.

Thanks to God for the divine wisdom and strength to carry us through our lives. Our prayer is that the contents of this book will help others reach a multitude of people as much as it has helped us reach the people that we have been blessed to touch.

Library of Congress Cataloging-in-Publication Data

Bennett, John Price, 1947-
    Rhythmic activities and dance / John Price Bennett, Pamela
Coughenour Riemer.
        p.   cm.
    Includes bibliographical references.
    ISBN 0-87322-718-2 (pbk.)
    1. Movement education.   2. Rhythm—Study and teaching (Elementary)
3. Dance for children—Study and teaching (Elementary)   4. Physical
education for children—Study and teaching (Elementary)   I. Riemer,
Pamela Coughenour, 1947-   .   II. Title.
GV452.B45   1995
372.86—dc20
                                                        94-38538
                                                        CIP

ISBN: 0-87322-718-2

Human Kinetics books are available at special discounts for bulk purchase. Special editions or book excerpts can also be created to specification. For details, contact the Special Sales Manager at Human Kinetics.

Printed in the United States of America   10   9   8   7   6   5

Human Kinetics
Web site: http://www.humankinetics.com/

United States: Human Kinetics, P.O. Box 5076, Champaign, IL 61825-5076
1-800-747-4457

Canada: Human Kinetics, 475 Devonshire Road, Unit 100, Windsor, ON N8Y 2L5
1-800-465-7301 (in Canada only)

Europe: Human Kinetics, P.O. Box IW14, Leeds LS16 6TR, United Kingdom
+44 (0)113-278 1708

Australia: Human Kinetics, 57A Price Avenue, Lower Mitcham, South Australia 5062
(08) 82771555

New Zealand: Human Kinetics, P.O. Box 105-231, Auckland Central
09-523-3462

CONTENTS

PREFACE

"To dance is to live and to live is to dance," according to Snoopy in the *Peanuts* comic strip. We have both spent our entire adult lives (and many of our childhood years) dancing to live and living to dance. Dance, as a cooperative activity, is truly the ultimate contact sport!

Possibly the greatest antidote to aging is physical activity. Dance can rejuvenate almost anyone. We should participate in some form of regular, fun-filled physical activity as a lifelong pursuit. Why not let the medium be dance? Dance offers a point of entry for students of all skill levels; dance is age appropriate and individually appropriate. In 1986 the National Association for the Education of Young Children (NAEYC) used just these criteria—suitable for the age and individual—to define "developmentally appropriate activity for children."

This book is the collaborative effort of two physical education teachers. We are each in our third decade of teaching and have taught the joy of dance to every age level. Each chapter of this book follows the guidelines of *Developmentally Appropriate Physical Education for Children*, a document produced by the Council on Physical Education for Children (COPEC) for the National Association of Sport and Physical Education (an association of the American Alliance for Health, Physical Education, Recreation, and Dance). *Developmentally Appropriate Physical Education for Children* is based on NAEYC's definition of developmentally appropriate activity.

I, John, grew up as an active child, playing a variety of sports, pursuing several forms of music, and dabbling in different types of dance. My first college dance class under Gladys Andrews Fleming opened a new world and taught me that everything we do has rhythm by nature and is potentially the basis for a dance. Pam Riemer, my coauthor, teaches dance to middle school students with high levels of success. Pam's program epitomizes a quality physical education program. Now, years after my initiation into the world of dance, Pam and I together have an opportunity to serve others in our profession, as Gladys Andrews Fleming served me.

We knew from the outset that this project would not resemble past efforts. We did not want a collection of activities or dances. This book will allow you, the teacher or prospective teacher, to introduce dance at a level appropriate to the individual skill levels of your students and to meet their needs. Each chapter is divided into three developmental levels to meet your student's needs: beginner, intermediate, and advanced. Each level identifies characteristics established in COPEC's *Developmentally Appropriate Physical Education for Children*. These characteristics serve as guidelines for progressing from one developmental level to another.

In *Rhythmic Activities and Dance*, we offer a resource for the physical education of our children. Dance as a component of K-8 programs can be a fun-filled experience promoting fitness for a lifetime. All rhythms and dance programs—whether beginning, continuing, or expanding—can benefit from fresh ideas. This book contains techniques and tips that can quickly lead you and your students to higher quality rhythmic activities and dance classes.

This book contains seven chapters and a resource section. It is designed to answer your questions about offering quality rhythmic activities and dance programs in your schools. It guides undergraduates and current teachers in developing their own rhythmic activities and dance programs.

Chapter 1 provides the background and direction for getting a rhythmic activities and dance program started. It includes planning, organization, and guidelines to prepare you to teach, to plan your units and lessons, and to manage your programs. This chapter lists cognitive, affective, and psychomotor characteristics, needs, and expectations for three grade levels: K-2, 3-5, and 6-8. Special features include three sample unit plans and three sample lesson plans for second, fifth, and eighth grades, rhythmic terms, and techniques to select partners and teach basic patterns. This chapter closes with sample instruments for evaluating both you and your students' performances.

Chapter 2 includes fun rhythmic games and movement activities that will introduce your students to rhythms. Many of the activities are familiar organizational patterns that have unusual rhythmic flavors and integrate various subject areas such as math, social studies, science, and language arts. Select from 28 activities across 4 categories: large-group, small-group, circuits, and games. They include basic locomotor movements for beginners, combination movements for intermediates, and selected dance steps for advanced students who are ready for more rhythmic challenges.

Chapter 3 provides a rhythmic aerobics and dance program that includes many variations. A sample aerobic workout includes warm-up activities, seven aerobic exercise routines, and a cool-down and stretch section. Guidelines on how to create your own aerobic routines and dances are provided, including how to read music and adjust movements to fit the music. Safety is emphasized within the 18 choreographed aerobic dance routines provided as examples. Challenge your more experienced students to create their own aerobic routines and dances.

The line dance chapter, Chapter 4, contains standard dances and examples of the current line dance craze. Because line dances are partnerless, they can assist greatly in the transition into dances with partners and be used as warm-ups for many sports. Select from 32 line dances across 3 developmental levels: beginner, intermediate, and advanced. Each level contains cognitive, affective, and psychomotor characteristics of learners to assist you in content decisions.

Chapter 5 introduces mixers that will bring students back wanting more. Mixers provide opportunities to meet and greet people in a very open, nonthreatening, warm environment that focuses on the individual. Virtually all cultures around the world have their own special mixers. Select from 30 mixers across 3 developmental levels: beginner, intermediate, and advanced.

The square dance and clogging chapter, Chapter 6, offers history and progresses through colorful moves and patterns that promote interest and success. The Appalachian Big Set uses a big circle formation to introduce square dance moves. It allows everyone to see each other, so they can learn from each other, and it provides a successful experience from the very beginning. Select from 44 square dance movements across 3 developmental levels: beginner, intermediate, and advanced. Six sample calls are provided as well as eight basic clogging steps.

Chapter 7, the chapter on folk dance, celebrates life and cultural diversity. Consider two levels of folk dance for your students: a modified one that permits early success and a patterned version that preserves the folk dance. This is an important consideration when implementing a child-centered approach, as this book does. Select from 32 folk dances across 3 developmental levels: beginner, intermediate, and advanced.

The opportunities for students of your rhythms and dance program to burst with energy are waiting. Try activities from all the chapters and then return to the areas that you and your students like the most. The last section of the book contains a helpful resource for obtaining more information. We want you to be successful with your students by increasing their self-confidence, self-image, and self-esteem through dance.

This book is not another list of every rhythmic activity needed in your K-8 rhythms and dance program. It is a blueprint to build your own developmentally appropriate rhythms and dance program—no matter your students' ages. Rather than the "how many dances can we teach" approach, we must teach principles and skills that promote a lifetime of fun-filled learning and fitness and that elevate students' confidence through physical activity. This book can be an instrument of inspiration. Use it in good health!

CHAPTER 1

STARTING YOUR RHYTHMIC ACTIVITIES PROGRAM

Everything you need for starting rhythmic activities with your dance program is included in one of the following topics in this chapter:

- Planning your program
- Unit planning
- Lesson planning
- Rhythmic terms
- Management
- Evaluation

PLANNING YOUR PROGRAM

Perhaps one of the most critical areas of program development is planning. To repeat a popular adage: Failing to plan is planning to fail. High-quality programs come from thorough preparation both in the planning stage and throughout implementation. The plan that you develop must be workable and user-friendly to be effective.

Many teachers of rhythm and dance in grades K-8 have had little preparation for teaching dance. Keeping this in mind, we built the planning section around three basic areas—program considerations, desired program outcomes, and class organizational concepts. Through the book we made every effort to assist you in developing your own programs, whatever your skill level.

Activities should be appropriate both to age and individual students. We divide characteristics generally according to three grade levels (K-2, 3-5, and 6-8), drawing the characteristics primarily from the National Association for Sports and Physical Education Outcomes Project and our experience.

You may discover that some of your students, regardless of age, are ready for different levels and challenges, based on their developmental stages. You can exercise judgment about moving to other levels in the book to ensure that what you offer your students is, indeed, developmentally appropriate.

The upcoming descriptions in general follow the characteristics, needs, and expectations of children at three different grade levels—K-2, 3-5, and 6-8—corresponding to beginner, intermediate, and advanced levels of progression (not skill levels).

Characteristics for Grades K-2

The student in grades K-2 will recognize and master basic movements and similarities between movements. In addition, at this level the child is able to identify feelings and derive high levels of joy from rhythm and dance movements.

Cognitive

- Recognize that practice is the way to skill development.
- Recognize that physical activity is important for personal well-being.
- Recognize that movement concepts are similar in a variety of skills.
- Identify appropriate behaviors in physical activities for participating with others.
- State reasons why safe and controlled movements are necessary.

Affective

- Identify feelings that result from participating in physical activities.
- Enjoy participation alone and with others.
- Look forward to physical activity lessons.
- Appreciate the benefits that accompany cooperation and sharing.
- Accept the feelings from challenges, successes, and failures in physical activity.
- Show consideration toward others in the physical activity setting.

Psychomotor

- Travel in different ways in a large group without bumping into others or falling.
- Travel forward and sideward and change direction quickly while responding to a signal.
- Demonstrate distinct contrasts between slow and fast speeds while traveling.
- Distinguish among straight, curved, and zigzag pathways while traveling in various ways.
- Combine various traveling patterns in time to the music.
- Skip, hop, gallop, and slide using mature motor patterns.
- Demonstrate safety while participating in any physical activity.

Characteristics for Grades 3-5

In grades 3-5, students will begin sequencing and recognizing differences between movements. More advanced movements are observed, and the role that students play in each other's rhythmic/dance activities becomes much more evident.

Cognitive

- Develop patterns and movement combinations into repeatable sequences.
- Identify how movement concepts can be used to refine movement skills.
- Identify activities that contribute to feelings of joy.
- Describe elements of mature movement patterns.
- Describe healthful benefits of regular and appropriate participation in physical activity.
- Design dance sequences that are personally interesting.
- Recognize that time and effort are prerequisites for skill improvement and fitness benefits.
- Recognize the cultural role of dance in understanding others.
- Detect, analyze, and correct errors in personal movement patterns.

Affective

- Appreciate differences and similarities in others' physical activity.
- Respect persons from different backgrounds and the cultural significance of the dances and rhythmic activities.

- Enjoy feelings from involvement in physical activity.
- Celebrate your own and others' successes and achievements.

Psychomotor

- Leap, leading with either foot.
- Develop movement patterns into repeatable sequences.
- Maintain aerobic activity for a specified time.
- Maintain appropriate body alignment during activity.
- Participate regularly in physical activity to improve skillful performance and physical fitness.
- Create and perform dances that combine traveling, balancing, and weight transfer with smooth sequences and intentional changes in direction, speed, and flow.
- Participate vigorously for a sustained time while maintaining a target heart rate.
- Monitor heart rate before, during, and after activity.

Characteristics for Grades 6-8

Students in grades 6-8 recognize the necessity for prerequisites in their movements and receive high levels of satisfaction from their performances. Sixth to eighth graders are much more fluid and creative in their routines than younger students, and they also demonstrate a much higher interest level in the performances.

Cognitive

- Recognize that time and effort are prerequisites for skill improvement and fitness benefits.
- Identify opportunities for regular physical activity.
- Identify training and conditioning principles.
- Identify the proper warm-up, conditioning, and cool-down skills and their purposes.
- Identify benefits from participating in various physical activities.
- Describe techniques using body and movement activities to communicate ideas and feelings.
- List long-term physiological, psychological, and cultural benefits of regular participation in physical activities.
- Describe training and conditioning principles for specific dances and physical activities.
- Describe appropriate personal and group conduct, including ethical and unethical behavior.
- Analyze and categorize activities according to the possible fitness benefits.
- Identify participation factors that contribute to enjoyment and self-expression.

Affective

- Identify, respect, and participate with persons of various skill levels.
- Exercise at home for enjoyment and benefits.
- Feel satisfaction from engaging in physical activities.
- Enjoy the aesthetic and creative aspects of performance.
- Respect physical and performance limitations of self and others.
- Desire to improve physical ability and performance.
- Enjoy meeting and cooperating with others during physical activity.

Psychomotor

- Recover from vigorous physical activity in an appropriate time.
- Correctly demonstrate activities to improve and maintain muscular strength and endurance, flexibility, and cardiorespiratory functioning.
- Participate in dance, both in and outside of school, based on individual interest and capabilities.
- Perform simple folk, country, and creative dances.
- Sustain aerobic activity, maintaining a target heart rate to achieve cardiovascular benefits.
- Improve and maintain appropriate body composition.
- Participate in an individualized fitness program.
- Perform dances with fluency and rhythm.
- Participate in dance activities representing various cultural backgrounds.

Remember to put a C.A.P. (cognitive, affective, psychomotor) on every lesson!

Program Considerations

There are four areas to consider when planning your program. They are the overall program goals, music selection, teaching environment, and equipment needs.

Overall Program Goals

While preparing for your classes, keep the following points of effective teaching in mind.

Preclass:

- Believe that all students can learn.
- Be a good time manager.
- Use a variety of instructional approaches, such as whole-group, small-group, direct teaching, discovery, guided practice, and cooperative learning.
- Have high expectations.

Review:

- Reinforce the concepts of previous lessons to support the newly learned activity.
- Praise the students.

Practice:

- Keep students on task.
- Diagnose the skill and ability you expect and prescribe solutions the child can use to improve.
- Interact with students in direct teaching.
- Be a skillful teacher because of your knowledge, preparation, and motivation.
- Provide clear feedback to individuals and to the group.
- Develop a climate conducive to learning (empathy, objectivity, individuality, etc.).

Evaluation:

- Acknowledge correct responses and teach to eliminate incorrect responses.

Music Selection

Music selection is a major issue and will require preparation time. In the beginning, select music that relates to your student's interests. Once the student is hooked, vary music selected to develop a variety of rhythmic dance skills. This will promote improvement in your student's overall movement. In choosing music, it is important to consider the lyrics and any negative connotations of the music.

The program should teach mastery of the rhythm basics. Mastering the basics will lead you and your students to success, skill development, and satisfaction.

Teaching Environment

You might have to deliver your program from a stage, in a cafeteria or gymnasium, on a blacktop, in a classroom, hallway, or any other place available in the school. Any of these facilities can work. Certainly, we'd all like our own multi-purpose room, dance room, or personal gymnasium, but we must adjust to what is available.

Remember, whatever teaching location you are given, it need not be a deterrent to delivering a rhythm and dance program at your school.

Equipment Needs

Everyone deserves a quality sound system for his or her programs. There is still a need to be able to play records, but this is diminishing rapidly. A cassette player (preferably dual-cassette) and a CD player are becoming more necessary. A microphone is critical, and a portable microphone is even better.

Desired Program Outcomes

When planning and conducting your rhythm and dance activities, include characteristics to facilitate effective classes. Compare your classes to the following list of attributes. The elements of a quality program should be present in effectively planned classes.

basic skills—Focus on the basics of rhythmic movement and a high level of mastery.

child-centered activity—The student is the focus of the lesson. Teach the child, not the lesson.

creativity—Students have the opportunity to create and are encouraged to go to higher levels of creativity.

fun—Everyone has a high level of enjoyment throughout the class. For success in your rhythms and dance class, create an atmosphere of fun.

safety—Safety is one of the most critical elements in an effective lesson. Avoiding an injury or unpleasant situation is a necessary ingredient for successful lessons.

self-esteem—Success builds more success and raises self-esteem. Students grow in a positive direction as their self-esteem grows.

self-evaluation—Lessons allow students to evaluate their own progress through a unit.

success—Every participant is successful on a regular basis throughout the lesson.

supplies—To maximize learning, supplies must be available for all students.

total involvement—Everyone is participating; no one is sitting out or waiting for a turn to be involved. Even numbers or an even split in sexes is not essential.

Keep these outcomes in mind when you develop your unit and lesson plans.

UNIT PLANNING

Unit planning is a basic component of the curriculum development process. However, prior to unit plan development is the development of your yearly plan. Decide how many lessons you will devote to games, gymnastics, and rhythm and dance activities during the year; then make your unit plans in these areas.

Unit size and length may be predetermined where you are teaching. Units are usually 3 to 9 weeks long. If a physical education program is integrated with dance concepts, dance may appear throughout the school year. Since integration enhances learning, every effort should be made to deliver your program this way. However, most dance programs are in blocks of 3 to 9 weeks, or 15 to 45 lessons. All units should include periodic evaluation throughout the program. Evaluation will be addressed later in this chapter.

Since lesson plans are developed from unit plans, they contain many of the same ingredients. The following is a suggested format for unit planning. Sample unit plans for the K-2, 3-5, and 6-8 grade levels are included to assist in your planning efforts. These grade levels correspond approximately to the beginner, intermediate, and advanced levels in this book.

| Sample Unit Plan Format |

Grade: Students' grade level

Goal(s): One to three statements about expected outcomes

Equipment: List of needed equipment

Area: Where the lesson is to be delivered

Safety: Special considerations for the unit

Activities: Make a daily outline that divides the lesson into three parts—opening, middle, and closing. Fill in your planned activities for that lesson. Remember that plans are only guidelines. It is useful to redo this unit plan before you use it again since it will change during the course.

A plan is critical for guiding your course of action. Without one you will go nowhere. The suggested activities and lesson plans in this chapter are described fully in the appropriate chapters.

K-2 Grade Level Sample 15-Lesson Unit Plan

Note: The rhythmic games and activities selected for this unit should focus on reviewing and mastering the locomotor movement patterns. Toward the end of the K-2 level, more students will have mastered the combinations and selected dance steps, so include them as a challenge. The actual dances in this unit, due to their simple steps and short length, are developmentally appropriate primarily for the K-2 grade level.

Second-Grade Sample Unit Plan

Goal(s):

1. The learner will develop rhythmic and dance skills in folk dance, line dance, and other rhythmic activities.
2. The learner will develop rhythmic and dance skills found in square dance.
3. The learner will create original dances using elements from folk dance, square dance, line dance, and other rhythmic activities.

Equipment: Sound system and musical selections

Area: Blacktop

Safety: Make sure the area is free of glass and rocks before each lesson.

Activities:

Day 1:
1. One Move After (p. 42) and Margie Dance (p. 87).
2. Clap and Stomp Three Times (p. 106) and Carnavalito (p. 154).
3. Big Circle (p. 35).

Day 2:
1. Down the Room in Waves (p. 36) and Follow the Leader (p. 39).
2. Introduce and practice these Big Circle Figures: positions (p. 125), Circle Left and Right, Forward and Back, Do-Si-Do, and the Swing (pp. 128-129).
3. Talking Drum (p. 45).

Day 3:
1. Partner Over and Under (p. 48).
2. Review and practice content from days 1 and 2, and introduce Danish Dance of Greeting (p. 155).
3. Broken Heart (p. 56).

Day 4:
1. Open Movement (p. 43).
2. Review Danish Dance of Greeting and Big Circle Figures to this point; add Big Circle Figures 5 through 8 (pp. 129-131).
3. Practice all calls.

Day 5:
1. Grids (p. 41).
2. Review and refine first four sessions.
3. Veins and Arteries (p. 57).

Day 6:
1. Agility Runs (p. 35).
2. Chimes of Dunkirk (p. 156) and Shoemaker's Dance (p. 158).
3. One Move After (p. 42).

Day 7:
1. Object Manipulation (p. 42).
2. Review Big Circle Figures to this point, and add Big Circle Figures 9 through 11 (p. 131).
3. Practice all Big Circle moves learned today.

Day 8:
1. Parts of Speech (p. 44).
2. Review Big Circle Figures to this point, and add Small Circle Figure 12 (p. 132).
3. La Candeliere (p. 157) and Margie Dance (p. 87).

Day 9:
1. Small Circles (p. 48).
2. Bouquet of Flowers and Scarf (p. 105) and Fun Mixers (p. 105).
3. Practice all Big and Small Circle Figures learned so far.

Day 10:
1. Friday Roll Call Jog and Dance (p. 41).
2. Review Small Circle Figure 12, and add Small Circle Figure 13 (p. 132).
3. Practice all Big Circle Figures.

Day 11:
1. Circuit 1 (p. 49).
2. Grapevine (p. 84) and Ruby Baby (p. 84).
3. Create a four-part line dance.

Day 12:
1. Fitness in America (p. 37).
2. Review Big and Small Circle Figures to this point, and add Small Circle Figure 14 (p. 132).
3. Refine line dances.

Day 13:
1. Eight, Four, Two (p. 36).
2. Jump Jim Jo (p. 157) and Seven Jumps (p. 159).
3. Review Big Circle Figures.

Day 14:

1. Four Wall (p. 40).
2. Review Big Circle Figures, and add Small Circle Figures 15 through 17 (p. 133).
3. Refine line dances.

Day 15:

1. Practice line dances in small groups.
2. Practice all Big Circle Figures.
3. Demonstrate line dance creations.

Three-Five Grade Level Sample 15-Lesson Unit Plan

Note: The rhythmic games and activities selected for this unit should focus on reviewing the locomotors, mastering the combinations, and introducing selected dance steps. The rhythms and dances in this unit have been suggested for the 3-5 grade level. They are appropriate here because the dance steps are more varied and the dance lengths have increased.

Fifth-Grade Sample Unit Plan

Goal(s):

1. The learner will develop rhythmic and dance skills in folk dance, line dance, and other rhythmic activities.
2. The learner will develop rhythmic and dance skills found in square dance.
3. The learner will create original dances using elements from folk dance, square dance, line dance, and other rhythmic activities.

Equipment: Sound system and musical selection

Area: Blacktop

Safety: Make sure the area is free of glass and rocks before each lesson.

Activities:

Day 1:

1. Four Wall (p. 40).
2. Electric Slide 1 The Boss (p. 92) and Circassian Circle (p. 109).
3. Run, Stop, Pivot (p. 45).

Day 2:

1. Four Corner Rhythms (p. 53).
2. Electric Slide 2 (p. 93) and western square dance; review of Big Circle Figures 1 to 5 (pp. 128-129).
3. Practice calls learned today.

Day 3:

1. Follow the Leader (p. 39).
2. Review and practice content from days 1 and 2, and add New York, New York (p. 90) to popular music.
3. Broken Heart (p. 56).

Day 4:
1. Countdown (p. 52).
2. New York, New York and western square dance; review Big Circle Figures 6 to 10 (pp. 130-131).
3. Practice calls learned today.

Day 5:
1. Four Wall (p. 40).
2. Review and refine first four sessions.
3. Veins and Arteries (p. 57).

Day 6:
1. Lines and Leaders (p. 47).
2. Patty-Cake Polka (p. 111) and Louisiana Saturday Night (p. 91).
3. Group Creation (p. 47).

Day 7:
1. Four Corner Rhythms (p. 53).
2. Review square dance movements 11 to 13 (pp. 131-132).
3. Practice moves learned today.

Day 8:
1. Circuit 1 (p. 49).
2. Review Big and Small Circle Figures to this point, and add Small Circle Figures 14 through 17 (pp. 132-133).
3. Bus Stop 1 (p. 92).

Day 9:
1. Circuit 2 (p. 50).
2. Ten Pretty Girls (p. 161) and Bunny Hop (p. 161).
3. Bus Stop 1 (p. 92).

Day 10:
1. Eight, Four, Two (p. 36).
2. Add Small Circle Figures 18 and 19 (p. 134).
3. Practice moves learned today.

Day 11:
1. Down the Room in Waves (p. 36).
2. Review Big and Small Circle Figures to this point, and add Small Circle Figures 20 through 22 (pp. 134-135).
3. Create a four- to eight-part line dance.

Day 12:
1. One Move After (p. 42).
2. Lucky Seven (p. 109) and Patty-Cake Polka (p. 111).
3. Refine line dances.

Day 13:
1. Rhythms Circuit (p. 55).
2. Review western square dance moves learned so far, and add Small Circle Figures 23 and 24 (pp. 135-136).
3. Practice movements learned today.

Day 14:
1. Veins and Arteries (p. 57).
2. Review and refine all western square dance movements learned so far.
3. Refine line dances.

Day 15:
1. Practice line dances in small groups.
2. Western square dance practice of all beginner level movements.
3. Demonstrate line dance creations.

Six-Eight Grade Level Sample 15-Lesson Unit Plan

Note: The rhythmic games and activities selected for this unit should focus on reviewing all locomotor and combination movements and mastering all the selected dance steps. The dances suggested for this unit are from those developmentally appropriate at the 6-8 grade level, based on pattern difficulty and dance length.

Eighth-Grade Sample Unit Plan

Goal(s):

1. The learner will develop rhythm and dance skills in folk dance, line dance, social dance, and other rhythmic activities.
2. The learner will develop rhythm and dance skills found in square dance.
3. The learner will create original dances using elements from folk dance, square dance, line dance, social dance, and other rhythmic activities.

Equipment: Sound system and musical selections

Area: Blacktop

Safety: Make sure the area is free of glass and rocks before each lesson.

Activities:

Day 1:
1. Four Wall (p. 40).
2. Sports Dance (p. 96) and Rise (p. 96).
3. Lines and Leaders (p. 47).

Day 2:
1. Four Corner Rhythms (p. 53).
2. DPI Special (p. 97) and Bus Stop 2 (p. 98).
3. Eight, Four, Two (p. 36).

Day 3:
1. Grids (p. 41).
2. Review western square dance movements 1 through 11 (Big Circle Figures) from the beginner level.
3. Practice all calls in review.

Day 4:
1. Circuit 2 (p. 50).
2. Review western square dance movements 12 through 24 (Small Circle Figures) from the beginner level.
3. Practice all calls in review.

Day 5:
1. Countdown (p. 52).
2. Rebel Strut (p. 98) and Texas Bop (p. 95).
3. Partner Over and Under (p. 48).

Day 6:
1. Follow the Leader (p. 39) and Wall Work (p. 46).
2. Review western square dance, and add movements 25 through 28 from the intermediate level (pp. 137-138).
3. Practice all square dance figures.

Day 7:
1. Small Circles (p. 48).
2. Farmer's Jig (p. 172) and Miserlou (p. 172).
3. Broken Heart (p. 56).

Day 8:
1. Object Manipulation (p. 42).
2. Review western square dance, and add movements 29 through 31 from the intermediate level (pp. 139-140).
3. Practice all square dance figures.

Day 9:
1. Rhythms Circuit (p. 55).
2. White Silver Sands (p. 115) and Teton Mountain Stomp (p. 117).
3. Practice western square dance movements.

Day 10:
1. Obstacle Courses (p. 54).
2. CJ Mixer (p. 117) and Tennessee Wig-Walk (p. 117).
3. Veins and Arteries (p. 57).

Day 11:
1. Virginia Reel (p. 170).
2. Cotton-Eyed Joe (p. 173).
3. Parts of Speech (p. 44).

Day 12:
1. Down the Room in Waves (p. 36).
2. Review western square dance, and add movements 32 and 33 from the intermediate level (p. 140).
3. Practice all square dance movements.

Day 13:

1. Run, Stop, Pivot (p. 45).

2. Review western square dance, and add movements 34 through 36 from the advanced level (pp. 141-142).

3. Create a four- to eight-part line dance.

Day 14:

1. Four Corner Rhythms (p. 53).

2. Review western square dance.

3. Refine line dance creations.

Day 15:

1. Review line dances, folk dances, mixers, and square dances taught during the unit.

2. Practice all western square dance movements.

3. Demonstrate line dance creations.

LESSON PLANNING

This section helps you get started with basic lesson planning. A description of the format for an individual lesson has been included. It is followed by sample lesson plans using this format with second, fifth, and eighth grades.

Individual lessons are usually 30 to 40 minutes with a beginning, middle, and closing. The beginning section sets the tone for the lesson, and it should have a lively focus on familiar or easy material. This section includes the focus, review, and objectives portions of the lesson. The middle section is the time for teaching new materials. A simple delivery is the "say, say and do, and do" method for teaching new material. Connecting the verbal cues to the movements tends to accelerate learning. In this part of the lesson, instruction and guided practice usually occur. An example would be for the teacher, when teaching a vine step to the right, to first say and do the movement, "Vine to the right by stepping right to the side, stepping left behind right, stepping right to the side, and touching left beside right." Next, the teacher would have the students say and do the vine to the right while the teacher continues to demonstrate. This time, however, only the key words, "Step, behind, step, touch," would be used. When students master this skill, they would stop saying the movements and simply do them. The closing section of the lesson is for application. Application should occur in a low-stress, high-success, fun-filled environment. This part of the lesson is devoted to independent practice and closure.

Decisions at this stage should reflect awareness of classroom conditions, such as class size and student ability levels, and should adhere to your unit objectives for the design and implementation of individual lessons. Thorough planning in the beginning will ensure success in your classes and high skill levels for your students.

This lesson plan format is straightforward and simple. It is followed by sample lesson plans at the second-, fifth-, and eighth-grade levels, and, again, these grade levels correspond approximately to the beginner, intermediate, and advanced levels found in the following chapter.

Sample Lesson Plan Format

Grade: Students' grade level

Goal(s) (Theme): One to three statements about expected outcomes

Objectives (Subthemes): State them in a familiar form. There will be three categories of objectives (subthemes)—cognitive, affective, and psychomotor. Use no more than three objectives in each category. The reason for this is to avoid getting so busy writing objectives that you miss the intent of the lesson.

Equipment: List of needed equipment

Area: Where the lesson is to be delivered

Safety: Special considerations for this lesson

PART A: (Opening) 5 to 10 minutes approximately—introduction and review to get students comfortable and interested. List and describe the activities with approximate times and include all special teaching cues for each activity.

PART B: (Middle) 10 to 20 minutes approximately—introduce new skills and rhythmic activities. List and describe the activities with approximate times and include all special teaching cues for each activity.

PART C: (Closing) 5 to 10 minutes approximately—culmination and application of the lesson. This is a time to practice skills, put together routines, or practice patterned activities in a nonthreatening, fun environment.

Second-Grade Sample Lesson Plan

Goal(s) (Theme): The students will put together the rhythmic movements necessary to perform a simple line folk dance and an American line dance.

Objectives (Subthemes):

Cognitive
The students will be able to describe the movements to Carnavalito and Eight Count.

Affective
The students will stay on task during the lesson.

Psychomotor
1. The students will be able to walk in a line, holding hands with someone on each side, to the beat of the music.
2. The students will be able to put together a sequence of eight different movements for a line dance.

Equipment: Sound system, music for Carnavalito and Eight Count

Area: Blacktop

Safety: Remind students to honor the spaces occupied by their classmates and not to enter occupied spaces.

PART A: (Opening) 8 minutes

Task Description:	Teaching Points:
Time: 3 minutes	
1. Rhythmic movement that focuses on basic locomotor patterns is put to music.	1. Remind students about safe use of space.

Time: 5 minutes

2. Four Corner Rhythms (p. 53)

2. No more than 12 people start in a corner. Students move at their own pace.

PART B: (Middle) 17 minutes

Task Description:	Teaching Points:

Time: 6 minutes

1. Give background on Carnavalito (p. 154).

1. Teach and practice dance having students walk to the music first and then hold hands in a line.

Time: 11 minutes

2. Discuss a different kind of line dance such as Eight Count (p. 84) and teach the eight steps.

2. Eliminate the turn when teaching this dance at this level.

Note: Make file cards or overheads with dance directions if you need them for your lesson.

PART C: (Closing) 5 minutes

Task Description:	Teaching Points:

Time: 5 minutes

1. Play Follow the Leader (p. 39) with new leaders every 30 seconds making up their own line dances to their selection of music.

1. Lines should be four or five students long.
2. Remind students about safe use of space.

Fifth-Grade Sample Lesson Plan

Goal(s) (Theme): The students will develop rhythmic skills that include locomotor and combination movements to enhance their physical, cultural, emotional, and social skills using selected mixers.

Objectives (Subthemes):

Cognitive
The students will be able to describe the sequences found in these mixers.

Affective
The students will respect the spaces occupied by other students.

Psychomotor
The students will demonstrate the rhythmic skills necessary for Paul Jones (p. 106) and Patty-Cake Polka (p. 111).

Equipment: PA system, record and cassette player, and music

Area: Blacktop

Safety: Honor other students' space.

PART A: (Opening) 10 minutes

Task Description:	Teaching Points:
Time: 10 minutes	
Four Wall (p. 40).	Introduce new steps in activity.

PART B: (Middle) 16 minutes

Task Description:	Teaching Points:
Time: 6 minutes	
1. Big Set Mixer (p. 107).	1. Try dance to both bluegrass music and popular music.
Time: 10 minutes	
2. CJ Mixer (p. 117).	2. Allow plenty of time on walk-through to learn the turns.

PART C: (Closing) 4 minutes

Task Description:	Teaching Points:
Time: 4 minutes	
Refine both dances.	Focus on good styling—posture, walking movements, etiquette with partners.

Eighth-Grade Sample Lesson Plan

Goal(s) (Theme): The students will develop rhythmic skills that include locomotor and combination movements to enhance their physical, cultural, emotional, and social skills using selected line dances.

Objectives (Subthemes):

Cognitive
The students will be able to describe the sequences found in these line dances.

Affective
The students will respect the spaces occupied by other students.

Psychomotor
The students will demonstrate the rhythmic skills necessary for Sports Dance (p. 96) and DPI Special (p. 97).

Equipment: PA system, record and cassette player, and music

Area: Blacktop

Safety: Honor other students' space.

PART A: (Opening) 10 minutes

Task Description:	Teaching Points:
Time: 10 minutes	
Four Corner Rhythms (p. 53).	Review old and introduce new steps for this activity.

PART B: (Middle) 14 minutes

Task Description:	Teaching Points:
Time: 7 minutes	
1. Sports Dance (p. 96)	1. Emphasize the connections to sport's movements.
Time: 7 minutes	
2. DPI Special (p. 97)	2. Go through the turn slowly several times.

PART C: (Closing) 6 minutes

Task Description:	Teaching Points:
Time: 6 minutes	
Eight, Four, Two (p. 36).	Use contemporary music that's "hot," or current, and teach all new steps.

Class Organizational Concepts

Put the fun back in the fundamentals! When introducing a rhythmic activity, it is appropriate to relate the activity to other areas of the curriculum, especially sports. Make connections for your students. Help them to see the connections. Point out previously learned steps or skills. In addition, give all the important background information that you know about a rhythmic activity to generate interest.

Several ingredients are essential to organizing an effective class. The following list is not all-inclusive, but with the other information in this chapter it becomes a helpful tool. As you plan your rhythmic activity classes, organize them around the following concepts:

cooperation and control—Cooperation and control are at a maximum when classes are well organized.

exploration—Give students an opportunity to experiment and explore.

individualization—Each person is able to participate as an individual.

problem solving—A productive method for learning new information is problem solving.

reinforcement to other areas—Reinforce other subject areas when teaching rhythmic activities. It should be an interdisciplinary adventure when appropriate.

self-awareness—Offer students the opportunity to build their levels of self-awareness in a nonthreatening environment.

self-discovery—A characteristic of all sessions is learning through self-discovery. Allow freedom to discover!

teacher as a guide—The teacher serves as a guide and not as a dictator.

RHYTHMIC TERMS

Basic terms for the text have been identified to assist you in your teaching endeavors. This section of rhythmic terms has four subsections.

The first describes the three major rhythmic components of any rhythmic, dance, or movement sequence. These three elements are the accent, rhythmic pattern, and basic pulse. The second subsection lists basic nonlocomotor and locomotor movements. The third subsection includes combinations of locomotor movements, thus the label, combination movements. The fourth subsection, "Selected Dance Steps," can assist you with dance steps that occur often in the K-8 dance program.

These four subsections provide the terminology and building blocks for your future program. Review them often to help your students become stronger and more confident dancers and rhythmic movers.

Rhythmic Elements

a. *Accent*—ranges from weak to strong, soft to heavy; the emphasis placed on a movement

b. *Rhythmic Pattern*—the duration of sounds, or movements and their relationship to silence, or the lack of movement; often emphasized by accent(s)

c. *Basic Pulse*—even, steady, and constant; the underlying beat

d. *Even Rhythmic Patterns*—sounds and/or movements that are performed with an equal amount of time between each sound and/or movement

e. *Uneven Rhythmic Patterns*—sounds and/or movements that are *not* performed with an equal amount of time between each sound and/or movement

Basic Movements

These include both nonlocomotor movements and locomotor movements. Nonlocomotor movements are usually done in place and do not move the whole body in and through space as do locomotor movements.

Nonlocomotor Movements

- Swinging
- Twisting
- Stretching
- Turning
- Bending
- Shaking
- Pushing
- Bouncing
- Pulling

Locomotor Movements

- Walking
- Running
- Jumping
- Hopping
- Leaping

Combination Movements

These are locomotor movements combined to form a new movement. The following combination movements represent those most often found in this book:

gallop (walk-leap)—An uneven rhythmic pattern, moving forward and backward using a step, close.

polka—An uneven rhythmic pattern (gallop and skip or slide and skip), moving forward, backward, sideward, and diagonally.

schottische—An even rhythmic pattern (walk, walk, walk, hop), moving forward, backward, sideward, and diagonally.

skip (walk-hop)—An uneven rhythmic pattern, moving forward, backward, sideward, and diagonally.

slide (walk-leap)—An uneven rhythmic pattern, moving sideward using a step, close.

two-step—This uneven rhythmic pattern (step-close-step; left, right, left or right, left, right; triple step, or step-ball-change) requires two counts of the music (1-and-2) to complete, moving forward, backward, sideward, and diagonally.

Selected Dance Steps

The cues given in these descriptions have been found the most beneficial to students. They are encountered with the greatest frequency when teaching dance at the K-8 levels.

bleking—Begin with feet together. Hop on the right foot and extend the left foot diagonally, with the heel touching the floor on count one; hop on the left foot diagonally, with the heel touching the floor on count two. Repeat and hold, alternating feet.

cha-cha-cha rhythm—Slow, slow, quick, quick, slow; counted 1, 2, 3-and-4. Basic is forward and backward, cha, cha, cha in place, and then backward and forward, cha, cha, cha in place.

Charleston—Walk forward on the left foot, kick or touch the right foot forward; walk backward on the right foot and touch the left foot back.

chassé-rock step—Slide to the right, stepping right, left, right, and place the left foot behind the right foot; rock backward on the left foot, and lift the right foot up then down, ending on the right foot. Slide to the left stepping left, right, left, and place the right foot behind the left foot; rock backward on the right foot, and lift the left foot up and down, ending on the left foot. (This step is counted 1-and-2, 3, 4.)

double Lindy and jitterbug—Left toe, step left, right toe, step right, step left back for a rock-step, using an even rhythm. One beat to each movement, counted 1, 2, 3, 4, 5, 6; girl does the opposite. A rock-step is a step backward, then a step forward in two counts. The girl does opposite footwork.

double Texas two-step—Two-step left and two-step right, walk left and right; counted 1 and 2, 3 and 4, 5, 6.

foot chugs—Scoot forward and backward on both feet without losing contact with the floor; do the same on either the right or left foot alone.

fox-trot or magic step—Slow, slow, quick, quick (slow, two beats, slow, two beats, quick, one beat, quick, one beat), step the left foot forward, step the right foot forward, step the left sideward a short step, close right to left and take weight on the right. The girl does opposite footwork.

grapevine and carioca—Step to right side on the right foot, step the left foot behind the right foot, step the right foot to side, touch the left in front of the right, repeat in multiples of four on both sides.

heel-toe polka—Also called *heel-toe, heel-toe with three slides*. Begin with feet together. Touch the right heel to the right diagonal with a slight hop, bring the right foot in front of the left foot, touch the toe, and hop. Repeat this twice, then slide right three times. Repeat this to the left side.

heel shuffles—Alternate touching the right and left heels forward.

hopscotch step—Begin with feet together. Jump from both feet to the left foot, bending the right knee and raising the right foot behind. Return to both feet and jump from both feet to the right foot, bending the left knee and raising the left foot behind.

hustle—Step to right side with the right foot, step behind the right foot with the left foot, step to right side with the right foot, kick with the left foot and clap. Repeat to other side.

jazz square walk—Walk forward on the right foot, step across with the left foot, walk backward on the right foot, backward on the left foot; alternate sides by changing the lead foot.

pivot step—Touch the left foot forward, keep the right foot in place, make a half turn (shifting weight from the left to the right foot). Repeat to face front again.

pony step—Begin with feet together. Step to the right side by stepping quickly right, left, right. Then step to the left side with left, right, left. Alternate right and left sides.

pull-downs—Lift arms above head, pull arms down as one knee is lifted. Repeat arm pull as the other knee is lifted.

rocker—Put weight forward on the right foot, then step backward on the left foot, alternating sides and directions.

sailor hop—Begin with feet together. Hop on the right foot three times to the right. On the fourth count, land on both feet, make a quarter turn back to the left with both feet together, knees bent slightly. Clap on the landing. Repeat to the left. Step to the right on the right foot and hop; step to the left on the left foot and hop; repeat the step-hops.

shag—The basic step is almost the same as a Triple Lindy except that styling is forward and backward instead of to the side. There are a number of variations from the basic. The basic is forward three, backward three, and rock-step, six counts total; counted 1 and 2, 3 and 4, 5, 6.

side touch—Touch the foot to the side, bring it back to the closed position, and step on it; alternate sides and forward and backward movement as well.

single Lindy—Step, step, rock; backward step, using an even rhythm.

step, behind, step, kick with three kicks—Begin with feet together. Step to the right, bring the left foot behind, step with the right foot, and kick with the left foot one time; then step with the left foot, kick with the right foot, step with the right foot, and kick again with the left foot. Repeat these eight counts on the opposite side.

step-hop, back step—Begin with feet together. Step right on the right foot and hop on the right foot. Step the left foot behind the right foot, weight changing to the left foot, and then step again on the right foot. Step left on the left foot and hop on the left foot. Step the right foot behind the left foot, weight changing to the right foot, and then step again on the left foot. Alternate sides.

step-kick—Step on the right foot, kick the left foot across; alternate sides.

step touch—Step right to the side and touch the left foot next to the right foot; alternate sides and forward and backward movement as well. Can modify the touch to be a kick.

Texas or Oklahoma two-step—Quick, quick, slow, slow, uneven rhythm; counted 1 (quick), 2 (quick), 3, 4 (slow), 5, 6 (slow).

Texas shuffle—Two-step left and two-step right; counted 1-and-2, 3-and-4.

three count—Two-step left and step on the right; counted 1-and-2, 3. The girl does the opposite.

triple Lindy—Left, step-close-step, right, step-close-step, left, rock-step, uneven rhythm; counted 1 and 2, 3 and 4, 5, 6. The styling is side-to-side with a drop-step backward. The girl does opposite footwork.

waltz—Three smooth walking steps on each beat of the music, counted 1, 2, 3.

ABBREVIATION MEANINGS AND FORMATION DIAGRAMS

There are several common abbreviations used to describe mixers, folk dance, and square dance. They are included here to assist you with your dances in these areas.

LOD = line of direction, counterclockwise (CCW)

RLOD = reverse line of direction, clockwise (CW)

CCW = counterclockwise

CW = clockwise

Marker = ▲

Run = − − −▶

Pivot =) or (

General movement direction, dancing, or walking = ⟶

Holding hands = ∧∧∧

Female* = ◑

Male* = ▷

Swing or turn = ↺

*Dark side indicates which direction the person faces.

Since so many dances have unique formations, a diagram of the basic formations (see Figures 1.1 through 1.10) has been included here to clarify meanings.

Figure 1.1 Double circle, men facing LOD.

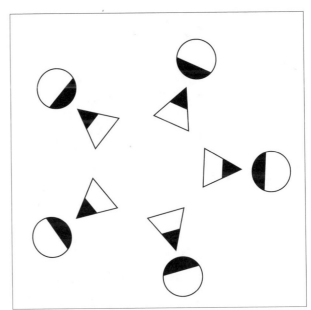

Figure 1.2 Double circle, men facing out.

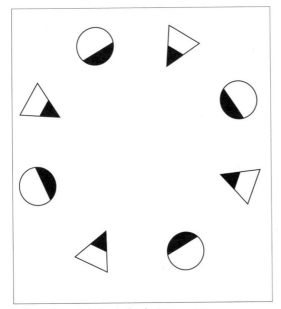

Figure 1.3 Single circle, facing center.

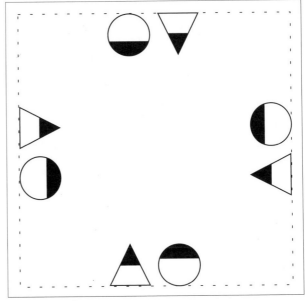

Figure 1.4 Square.

Figure 1.5   Sets of three, facing CCW.

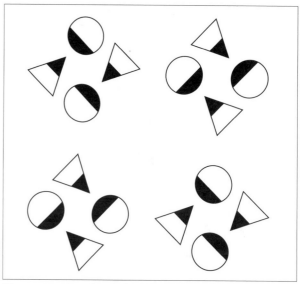

Figure 1.6   Double circle with two couples, facing each other.

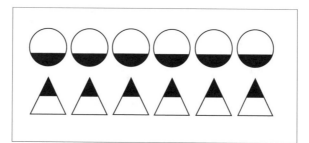

Figure 1.7   Longways set.

Figure 1.8   Single circle, partners facing.

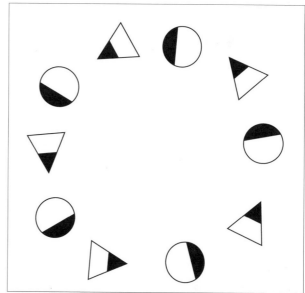

Figure 1.9   Single circle, facing LOD.

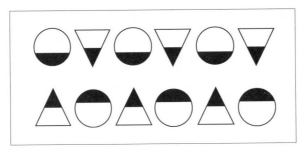

Figure 1.10   Duple improper contra set.

MANAGEMENT

Two considerations must be addressed in the planning process for a rhythm and dance unit. These questions are, "How can my students select their partners in a nonthreatening way?" and, "How do I prefer to teach the steps of a particular dance?" There are many ways to answer these questions. However, we have included a method for selecting partners, called "connect and disconnect," and another method for teaching steps, called the "seat-to-feet method." These are two possibilities for accomplishing these tasks.

Selecting Partners—Connect and Disconnect

Children's social and developmental needs are not always met in school; therefore, social development must be undertaken in the classroom. Rhythmic activities are a wonderful vehicle for this. The following method can take the trauma out of socializing.

When you ask students to get a partner and hold hands, you may have asked them to do the worst thing in the whole wide world. Therefore, it is important to make getting a partner a grand thing to do.

Invite the students to sit on the floor in a cluster, not in any specific formation. Ask them to define the word "connect." Then ask the students to define "disconnect." Now let the students demonstrate the terms. Have one student turn to a classmate and ask him or her to connect their index fingers only. This becomes their number one connection. Ask them to disconnect their index fingers. (Holding hands is not "cool," especially in grades 6-8. You have remedied that problem by not asking them to hold hands, but you have allowed them comfortably to identify a partner.)

The class is now ready for the adventure of connecting with a specific person without holding hands. If there are an uneven number of students, allow one group to have a connection with three students. This way NO ONE is left out or embarrassed. Say aloud, "Connect number one," and the students will find a partner immediately. Say aloud, "Disconnect," and the students will disconnect their index fingers. Make sure that the students remember who their number one connections are.

Now say aloud, "Connect number two," and the students are to find a new connection and touch their index fingers. This activity can continue until you have as many connections as you have activities.

What will you do with these connections? Begin teaching rhythmic activities. Turn on the music for the connection number one partners, and have them do an activity such as cross-clapping their hands. Using the music "Never Gonna Let You Go" by Rick Astley, you can have five or six activities, such as these:

- **Connect number one**—Cross-Clapping their hands (clap as many times as necessary to make the connection).

- **Connect number two**—Cross-Kicking their legs (kick as many times as necessary to make the connection).

- **Connect number three**—Elbow Swing four counts one way and reverse direction.

- **Connect number four**—Cha-Cha with a boy–girl combination.

- **Connect number five**—The Bump: swinging their hips and the bump connects the hip (swing and bump as many times as necessary to make the connection).

The concept of connection lets you teach many skills, using equipment (balls, hoops, scarves, etc.) as well as basic or creative movement.

Choosing partners this way is effective for allowing children to get to know the students in their class. Working together is necessary in our society. This system gives all children the opportunity to be with a partner they might not have chosen. Since they are partners for a very short time, they can learn to be comfortable with many other students.

The method allows the change of partners, or connections, to be very brief and constant so the students realize they will not be "stuck" with a particular connection. This is often the reason children do not like to choose partners.

The process is a grand memory exercise. Use the music, "Memory," fast edition, to practice this connect and disconnect activity and to emphasize remembering the connections. Add some combinations: boy–girl combination, three-person combination, four-person combination, two boy–two girl combination, and so on. This will involve the children in paying attention to directions and not to potential partners. They will be eager to get anyone to connect so they get the task right and please the teacher.

Make this a fun adventure, and it will be a wonderful experience for both students and teacher.

Teaching Rhythmic Steps and Movements—Seat-to-Feet Method

A child might avoid learning rhythmic activities, saying, "I can't do it because it's too hard," "I don't want to look silly in front of my friends," "I'm too embarrassed," or "That's stupid." Whatever the excuse, it comes from the same source: a lack of self-confidence and security. If you ask adults why they haven't become comfortable enough to perform rhythmic and dance activities in front of others, you will hear the same reasons.

With the seat-to-feet method of learning rhythmic activities, these reasons evaporate: Students start by sitting on the floor in a cozy cluster to ensure security.

Then they clap the rhythm of the activity that we wish to teach: The students sit on the floor, clapping to the music. Next they snap their fingers to the rhythm.

Let them practice to the beat and get used to it. They will be much more successful if they first spend time learning the rhythm; they can then concentrate on the steps.

Once the hand-clapping session is successful, ask the students to keep time to the music with their feet. They are still sitting in a scattered formation, so the threat of being awkward is absent. They keep time with the music by having each foot represent a beat and by alternating feet from right to left or left to right. Which foot leads, or starts, has little significance at this point: You are trying to teach a rhythm and increase self-confidence, not teach a dance step. The students should practice with the music until they feel comfortable. You will probably see a high level of success. Walk around to accustom them to your being present to help and encourage them, not to bring attention to or embarrass them in front of their friends. If you present this step correctly, the students will feel challenged to be truly successful, and they will try even harder.

The next phase is "sneaking up" on the standing portion of the process. Have the students come up on their knees, clap to the music, and then snap their fingers to the music. Because they were successful with the clapping and snapping session, they will gladly come to their knees to try something new. They now have the background and self-confidence to want to try each challenge as an adventure.

At last it is time to stand up. Rather than the students standing up, waiting to start the rhythm, have them stand up *while* they are clapping. Then change the clapping to snapping—the change will not be as noticeable. As soon as all students are up, they can begin keeping time with their feet. They will be at ease at this point, because it is familiar and they have been successful at it.

They are ready to learn any basic rhythmic dance step that you wish. Remember to start them with their seat on the floor, and to gradually let them stand with their feet on the floor.

Keep in mind that you teach the children—not the lesson. Get the kids comfortable on their seats. They will begin asking to go on. Get them eager to move forward. This may take more time than you feel comfortable taking, but you will surely save time and accomplish more in the long run.

Using key words, such as *slow* and *quick*, will help the students get the correct rhythm with their dance steps and also help them differentiate the various dances. For example, while teaching the Cha-Cha, recite "slow, slow, quick, quick, quick." While teaching the Waltz, recite "slow, quick, quick"; for the Fox Trot, "slow, slow, quick, quick"; for the Tango, "slow, slow, quick, quick, slow"; for the Shag, "quick, quick, quick, quick, quick, quick, slow, slow."

Have the kids move around the room doing the rhythmic pattern in all directions. Having established a sense of success with the connect and disconnect, you can now tell them to connect number one and do this rhythmic pattern with their connections. At this point, it doesn't matter which foot or direction they use. This is when the children may be creative, experience success, and feel grandeur! If they can do it with a "like" connection, they will slip into another connection—the boy–girl combination. Why? Because they have the self-confidence that they can do it and feel the security of success.

EVALUATION

As with all activity and teaching, evaluation is critical to future success in your classes. Rhythmic activities appear more subjective than they actually are. It is possible to remove some of this subjectivity and to collect information.

Rhythmic activities should be evaluated regularly. Students need regular feedback, as does the teacher. Two instruments follow to assist you in this effort. The first one serves as a self-evaluation of you, the teacher. It is a Likert-type scale format, and you should average 3 or better on all items throughout the year. It will provide you with feedback about how you are doing in the classroom. The second instrument provides feedback to your students about their rhythmic activity performances and gives you a more definitive assessment for grading. It is designed to provide a rhythmic skill's analysis for the student. The scoring on the second instrument is based on 50 points with a 5-point bonus for higher quality performance. This score can be doubled for a final score of 100. The test can be used again for a second try or a second rhythmic activity.

While the second instrument can be used to make specific grades, it can also allow students the opportunity to evaluate themselves and classmates during a unit. It may be more useful as a pretest, middle, and posttest. However you use these two instruments, remember the value of building evaluative techniques into your regular program.

Self-Evaluation—A Key to Effectively Teaching Rhythms

Growth comes through self-evaluation and willingness to change. The checklist on pages 29 and 30 is designed to assist in this self-evaluation process and to help students perform at higher levels. It has been modified for the teaching of rhythmic and dance activities. Use it to see how you are doing in the rhythm and dance classroom.

Suggested Student or Teacher Evaluation

The sample Rhythmic Assessment Form on page 30 can provide a wealth of information to both students and teachers when used in the classroom. It can be used as a repetitive measure or on a one-time basis. Teachers can do the assessment, or students can use the instrument on themselves or other students. It can put a numerical value on student activity and assist the teacher in evaluating what is taking place relating to the cognitive, affective, and psychomotor aspects of development. However, the items to be evaluated should be designed to meet the specific needs of your classes. The strength of this instrument lies in the flexibility of selecting or developing items conducive to your program. The items can be given numbers from 1 to 10 or 1 to 5. Another suggestion would be to use either an "s" for satisfactory or a "u" for unsatisfactory when evaluating the performances of your students. Whatever you decide, implementing regular assessments will provide another opportunity for growth within your classes.

The opportunities for the rhythmic and dance portion of your K-8 programs to burst with energy are waiting for you in this book. Try activities from all the chapters and then return to the areas that you and your students like the most. The last section of the book contains a helpful resource list to answer any questions you have about your own rhythmic and dance program.

Rhythm and Dance Checklist

I use ability grouping to meet individual needs and provide maximum learning opportunities for all in my rhythm and dance classes.

Always   5   4   3   2   1   Never

I use screening tests, both formal and informal, to assess strengths and weaknesses of students regarding fitness and basic rhythmic skills and as a guide to planning activities to help students improve.

Always   5   4   3   2   1   Never

I help organize Individualized Educational Plans for students categorized as having special needs in learning rhythms.

Always   5   4   3   2   1   Never

I maximize supplies, equipment, and facilities to keep every student engaged in activity.

Always   5   4   3   2   1   Never

I use small-group activities or centers so students don't have to wait to be active.

Always   5   4   3   2   1   Never

I have added a new activity to the curriculum for each grade I will teach rhythms and dance to this year.

Always   5   4   3   2   1   Never

I do not repeat the same rhythmic and dance activities without a change in approach or scope.

Always   5   4   3   2   1   Never

I decorate my teaching area with educational bulletin boards, floor patterns, pictures, and a new vocabulary for rhythm and dance.

Always   5   4   3   2   1   Never

I involve older students in assisting younger students with supply maintenance, special events, clubs, or programs related to rhythms.

Always   5   4   3   2   1   Never

I belong to my professional organization and keep abreast of new methods and materials in the rhythm and dance area.

Always   5   4   3   2   1   Never

I communicate with the staff about dance education experiences and related issues.

Always   5   4   3   2   1   Never

I am a resource to my staff and community regarding community activities to enhance fitness.

Always   5   4   3   2   1   Never

Low scores on individual items indicate a need for fuller evaluation of a particular aspect of your program. Further evaluation may eventually lead to changes in your methods of teaching.

Rhythmic Assessment Form

Student's Name_____

Cognitive Evaluation:

_____ 1. Recognizes the count being used.

_____ 2. Understands the concept and pattern used in the dance.

_____ 3. Understands the concepts of following and leading indications.

_____ 4. Understands styling concepts.

_____ 5. Understands the concept of presenting the dance.

_____ 6. Understands the concept of rhythm.

Affective Evaluation:

_____ 1. Can maintain own working space.

_____ 2. Can mirror a partner or leader without teaching.

_____ 3. Can work with a partner on the footwork.

Psychomotor Evaluation:

_____ 1. Can clap to the various rhythms of the dance.

_____ 2. Can lead and follow.

_____ 3. Can display the proper footwork for the dance.

_____ 4. Can distinguish and demonstrate the styling for the dance.

_____ 5. Can demonstrate the rhythm of the dance.

_____ 6. Can present the dance.

SUMMARY

This chapter has focused on starting your rhythm activities program, rhythmic components, basic terms and formations, classroom management, and evaluation. In-depth unit and lesson planning guidelines and samples were included in the chapter, along with specific suggestions on how to make teaching easier, to assist you in developing your own program. Student and self-evaluations were provided to guide you, your students, and your program in the future. This evaluation process supports student assessment and participation, is nonthreatening, and helps to promote the joy of learning rhythm and dance. Striving to adhere to the content if this chapter will help ensure that your program is balanced and fulfills the developmental needs of every student.

CHAPTER 2

RHYTHMIC GAMES AND ACTIVITIES

This chapter of rhythmic activities is designed for you, the teacher of rhythmics and dance. It is intended to introduce rhythms and dance movements in a no-fault, nonthreatening atmosphere to students at the K-8 grade levels.

Many opportunities are provided to reinforce and improve the basic skills needed for rhythmic activities and dance. The activities will assist your dance program, while stimulating students to develop at their own pace. Dance skills can be enhanced when a student's anonymity is maintained and the students do not recognize that they are working on dance skills. The activities in this chapter will motivate your students to work on dance skills without any risk of embarrassment.

As you begin using these activities, you will notice opportunities to integrate subjects such as math, social studies, science, and language arts with your physical education classes. Take advantage of these connections and help your students see them as well.

Counting, adding, and subtracting occur in Eight, Four, Two, in the circuits, and in Countdown. Games like Broken Heart and Veins and Arteries provide teachers with an opening to examine some basics of the physiology of exercise with their students. Fitness in America could lead to a lesson in social studies. Parts of Speech or Partner Over and Under allows language arts to be integrated with our teaching in the physical education classroom. These activities are the obvious places to integrate material. The only limitations for integration are those we place on ourselves.

You will recognize familiar activities as well as a variety of new ones to expand your students' dance skills. All are designed to promote the development of dance skills and fitness. The familiar activities have been reshaped into dance-related fitness activities. This new look to old activities makes them appealing for all age groups. Allow your students an opportunity to add new ways to integrate. The feeling of ownership makes students feel important.

FROM OLD TO NEW

Although you will recognize many of these activities immediately, look closely because they may not be what you think they are. Each one has been modified with a focus on the elements of dance. Each one reinforces dance skills and fitness simultaneously. Whether the changes appear small or large, you will be able to focus on new directions through some old organizational patterns.

This chapter is arranged into four categories—large-group, small-group, circuit types of activities, and games. The large-group activities may lead to high-quality movement as do the small-group activities depending on how you use them. The circuits provide opportunities to practice dance skills in nonthreatening environments, and the games move to a higher level application of a rhythmic dance activity.

Within these four categories are many activities that will be appropriate for your program. You can enliven your classes by applying basic dance skills using new and challenging conditions. Use these activities and modify them to your needs. With slight changes, you could move one to a different category.

The activities are listed below in their respective groups. The individual descriptions follow. Try them as openings and closings to your lessons. They may fit the middle of your lessons, depending on your focus in a particular lesson. When you are working with the K-2 (beginner) level, the focus will be on the locomotor basics of walking, running, leaping, jumping, and hopping in a rhythmic manner. When these have been mastered, you will move to the combination moves listed in chapter one—skipping, sliding, galloping, doing the polka, and so on. When you are teaching the 3-5 (intermediate) grade level, your focus will be first on the combination movements, then shift to the selected dance steps suggested in chapter 1. At the 6-8 (advanced) grade level, the focus shifts to mastery of the selected dance steps found in the first chapter.

As you are selecting activities from this chapter for your program, be aware of this progression.

LIST OF ACTIVITIES IN THIS CHAPTER

We list here all the fitness activities in this chapter, dividing them into four groups (large-group activities, small-group activities, circuits, and games) to facilitate using them in your programs.

MUSIC SELECTION

Selecting music is a critical element in all the following activity descriptions. Each activity is designed to improve the students' rhythm and dance development. The intent is to increase overall coordination, agility, stamina, and power to maximize and ensure total physical development. It is the combination of rhythmic movement with fitness activities that raises motivation and frees movement more than many other fitness activities. Different tempos and types of music will promote and provide different levels of development.

To get them "hooked" on the activity, select music in the beginning that students will like. Later you can vary the music to enhance the overall quality of your students' movements. Getting the participants hooked on an activity is the critical element. Always remember this analogy when selecting music: When you go fishing, do you bait the hook with what you want or what the fish wants? Selecting music is similar. Once you've hooked the audience, you can play it anyway you like. You can take everyone on a journey to being a better, more balanced, and confident mover.

As you introduce these activities in your program, be sure to select rhythmic movements that are developmentally appropriate for your group of students. Basics are basics. (Refer to the section on rhythmic terms in chapter 1 for a refresher.) Begin with locomotor movements, progress to combination movements, and then select dance steps to use in your lessons. Following this progression will ensure entry level for all students and higher levels of mastery with all your students in the rhythmic dance movements.

As your students improve, vary the tasks in directions, extensions, props, partnering, and groups as is appropriate. This will enhance your students' growth in rhythmic dance skills.

LARGE-GROUP ACTIVITIES

The selection of large-group activities here should fill the needs of your classes. We have chosen these activities and modified them primarily to provide your students with activities to help develop total fitness and learn or reinforce a variety of dance skills.

1. Agility Runs

Goal: Students match their movements to the rhythms in and out of markers or between lines, using many different dance movements with varied effort qualities.

Formation: Determined by the design of activities

Procedure: This activity is done in and out of markers or between lines, with different dance movements and effort qualities of movement (see Figure 2.1). It is a low-cost activity with a high return. By using some locomotor, combination, and dance steps from the rhythmic terms section in chapter 1, students will find Agility Runs become more challenging. They can greatly increase growth long term.

Teaching Tip: Provide rhythmic accompaniment for the movements, particularly music that students can strongly relate to and with rhythms they can match their movements to.

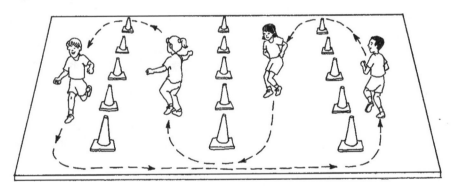

Figure 2.1   Students running Agility Runs.

2. Big Circle

Goal: Students experience large-group participation and develop a variety of dance skills.

Formation: Students form a big circle holding hands and move as directed (see Figure 2.2).

Figure 2.2   The Big Circle here moves clockwise.

Procedure: Give cues for movements that build around the rhythmic terms. Also, as in the previous activity, add music that will elicit different types of movements from your students.

Teaching Tip: Direct students to circle left and right, move in and out, and change tempos as you choose, for each situation.

3. Down the Room in Waves

Goal: Students improve locomotor and combination movements with and without equipment while combining sports skills with dance movements.

Formation: Students are lined up along one side of a room.

Procedure: Move the length of the room in large waves (see Figure 2.3). Practice locomotors, combinations, and other dance steps the length of the room. Include equipment such as balls and ropes. Encourage students to make up variations on the basics. Don't forget to combine sports skill movements with dance movements.

Teaching Tip: Focus on basic locomotors at the K-2 level, combinations at the 3-5 level, and selected dance steps at the 6-8 level.

Figure 2.3   In Down the Room in Waves students can choose, among other things, to hop, slide, run, walk, or gallop.

4. Eight, Four, Two

Goal: Students experience large-group participation and develop a variety of dance skills.

Formation: Students are spread out in the room with everyone facing the front.

Procedure: After a designated dance movement is performed eight times, everyone makes a quarter turn right and repeats the movement eight times (see Figure 2.4). Repeat with a quarter turn right (students now facing the back of class), and again with a quarter turn right. When the students make one more quarter turn to face the front, repeat all movements four times, and follow the preceding sequence. Then repeat the movements two times through the entire sequence, thus the name Eight, Four, Two.

Teaching Tip: Use any number of movements from one move to several. Let students contribute suggestions for the activity and bring their own music. Always use music. Post moves for the day on the third wall that the group faces, so they can continue without stopping.

Suggested Moves: Begin with basic locomotor, then combinations, then the selected dance steps from the first chapter. This would be the progression to follow when organizing your program.

Figure 2.4   Students start facing front wall and do 8 repetitions before making a quarter turn right.

Basic Locomotor

- Walk
- Run
- Leap
- Jump
- Hop

Combination

- Slide and lunge
- Gallop and leap
- Skip and jump
- Polka and turn

Selected Dance Steps

- Step touches
- Grapevines
- Pivots
- Push-ups
- Knee lifts
- Sit-ups or crunches
- Bleking steps
- Schottische
- Lunges
- Cha-Cha
- Lindy steps
- Jazz circles
- Jazz walk

5. Fitness in America

Goal: Students participate in an interdisciplinary unit with social studies, language arts, economics, math, and science. Students can learn states and their spellings, their capitals, poetry alliterations, science terms, classical music appreciation, creative imagining of terrain, as well as a variety of dance movements. The exercises are to be interpreted by the students, and they may do them under the guidance of the teacher.

Formation: Students set up stations representing the states. The class is presented as a circuit training unit.

Procedure: The directions for this activity are very flexible. Each student stays at the station for a specific time, from 1 to 3 minutes. Classical music with this activity is a great motivator and helps to incorporate cultural arts into the physical education program. Each student can draw a state, cut it out, and mount it on a piece of cardboard. The students can draw what the state produces, label the state's important areas, its capital, its recreation facilities, and its professional athletic teams. These visual aids widen the scope of the student's education by integrating physical education with other aspects of the curriculum.

Teaching Tips: Listed below are the states and what can be done at each station (see Figure 2.5). This activity allows you to introduce classical music into the physical education curriculum. The *Hooked on Classics* collection is ideal for Fitness in America.

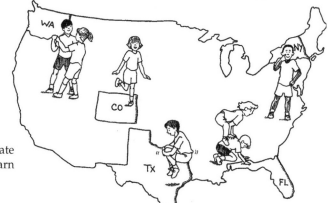

Figure 2.5 Playing Fitness in America helps students associate movements with states and learn state names.

Suggested Moves: The names beside each state simply serve as a starting point. They promote problem solving by allowing the students to create the movements. The names serve only as stimulators of ideas. The students will develop the movements and later create new names as well. Maybe the students could create a motion that indicates a state product, or act out the recreational activity for which the state is noted. The student could display the state's shape by walking out its outline. There are many activities that could be incorporated into Fitness in America. It could be used in every grade level, making the activity simple or complex, as necessary. Children will have ideas that will inspire more excitement and spontaneity in their actions. Let the children create and be free.

Alabama Arm Crosses
Alaska Alley Cat Leaps
Arizona Airplanes
Arkansas Arm Circle
California Cancan
Colorado Charleston
Connecticut Crunches
Delaware Dips
Florida Frog Leaps

Georgia Gallops
Hawaii High Kicks
Idaho Idle Walk
Illinois Indian Walks
Indiana Indy Jogs
Iowa Inverted Push-Up
Kansas Kicks
Kentucky Karate Kicks
Louisiana Lunges

Maine Motor Bikes
Maryland Mambo
Massachusetts Magic Step
Michigan Muscle Man
Minnesota Mini Kicks
Mississippi Mash Potatoes
Missouri Moon Walks
Montana Mountain Climbers
Nebraska Knee Lifts
Nevada Knee Bends
New Hampshire Nervous Jumps
New Jersey Neck Stretchers
New Mexico Nonsense Walks
New York Nose Wiggles
North Carolina Knuckle Bends
North Dakota Knee Slaps

Ohio Over and Under
Oklahoma Over Jumps
Oregon Over Flows
Pennsylvania Push-Ups
Rhode Island Rope Jumper
South Carolina Standing Scale
South Dakota Sit-Ups
Tennessee Toe Touches
Texas Tuck Jumps
Utah Umbrella Turns
Vermont Vertical Jumps
Virginia V-Sits
Washington Waltz
West Virginia Waves
Wisconsin Wind Mills
Wyoming Waddles

Music Suggestions: The Royal Philharmonic Orchestra, *The Best of 'Hooked on Classics'*, K-Tel International (USA), 247-4.

The Royal Philharmonic Orchestra, *Hooked on Classics*, K-Tel International (USA), NU 6114.

The Royal Philharmonic Orchestra, *Hooked on Classics 2 Can't Stop the Classics*, K-Tel International (USA), NU 6894.

The Royal Philharmonic Orchestra, *Hooked on Classics 3 Journey Through the Classics*, K-Tel International (USA), 626-4.

6. Follow the Leader

Goal: Students learn the basics, then gradually develop the more complex dance steps.

Formation: One large group, small groups, or partners move around the room and change the effort qualities (time, force, space, and flow) of their dance movements according to your directions (see Figure 2.6).

Figure 2.6   The teacher as leader in Follow the Leader.

Procedure: Everyone can follow you, or several leaders can be selected. Change leaders when you feel it is appropriate.

Teaching Tip: When using this activity in the lower grade levels, focus on the basics, then gradually move to the more complex dance steps.

7. Four Wall (This activity is a variation on Eight, Four, Two.)

Goal: Students experience large-group participation and develop a variety of dance skills.

Formation: Students go into the room and start walking, jogging, or practicing a dance step.

Procedure: On your signal to begin, students move to the center of the room and face the front wall—wall A (see Figure 2.7). Begin at level A1 with medium-speed music (120 beats per minute or BPM). On your signal, students turn to face the wall on their right—wall B, and do the activity for level B1. Continue turning right on the signal, and move down the list C1, D1, A2, B2, etc., until you complete them, or you want to stop.

Teaching Tip: Start with the basic locomotors, then progress through the movements as previously described.

Figure 2.7   Four Wall allows your students to explore many levels of dance and movement.

Suggested Moves:

Wall A

A1—Step Touch

A2—Jazz Square going both left and right

A3—Skip

A4—Double Lindy

Wall B

B1—Step-Kick

B2—Slide

B3—Schottische

B4—Triple Lindy

Wall C

C1—Side Touch

C2—Gallop

C3—Two-Step

C4—Shag

Wall D

D1—Heel Shuffle

D2—Run

D3—Cha-Cha

D4—Fox Trot

8. Friday Roll Call Jog and Dance

Goal: Students see how many minutes of dance or how many laps they can run while waiting for class to start.

Formation: Students do a 5- to 10-minute run or dance for their warm-up (see Figure 2.8).

Procedure: When it is time to stop, have students respond with the number of laps or the amount of time that they ran or danced on each Friday.

Teaching Tip: Let students keep their own records of the number of laps they ran or the amount of time they danced.

Figure 2.8 Having students play a game instead of waiting around at the start of a class period gives them an incentive to get on task quickly.

9. Grids

Goal: Students maximize all components of development in the dance and games skill areas.

Formation: Grids are squares 20 to 30 feet on a side marked off with cones or lines (see Figure 2.9).

Figure 2.9 Grids provide excellent boundaries for personal or group choreography.

Procedure: Students move according to the task you set. Squares can be either used by individual students or shared by more than one student. The tasks follow the familiar progression from basic to the more complex movements. In the lower grades start with the locomotors, go to the combinations, then to the selected dance steps.

Teaching Tip: Review the basics at all grade levels.

10. Object Manipulation

Goal: Students use dance moves in and through the teaching station with an object—balls, ropes, hoops, beanbags, or ribbons.

Formation: Determined by the design of the teaching stations

Procedure: Vary the tasks you ask the students to perform. For example, first ask the students to move directly through the open spaces in the teaching station while dribbling a ball; second, ask them to move indirectly through the open spaces while dribbling the ball (see Figure 2.10).

Teaching Tip: By varying the elements of time, force, space, and flow the movement task can be given a new meaning.

Figure 2.10   Object Manipulation has a flexible formation, and it can be tailored to your methods of teaching.

11. One Move After

Goal: Students at the K-2 level master the basic locomotors and as many of the combinations as possible; at the 3-5 level, students master the combination movements and some of the selected dance steps; at the 6-8 level, students master all the previous material and as many of the selected dance steps as possible.

Formation: Open

Procedure: Either you or a student leader repeats a dance pattern several times, then stops. The group begins performing this movement. The leader starts a second dance movement. When the leader begins a third dance movement, the group switches to the second movement. This continues for as long as you want (see Figure 2.11). The activity gets its name because the group is always doing the move after the leader has completed it. This is a great activity for introducing movements, reviewing movements, and promoting leadership in your classes.

Teaching Tip: Use a variety of music to promote a wide range of rhythmic movements.

Figure 2.11   Students do hops while the teacher introduces skips.

12. Open Movement

Goal: Students demonstrate quality movement in and through the open spaces of the teaching station.

Formation: Open

Procedure: You direct nonlocomotor, locomotor, combination, and dance movements through the entire teaching area (see Figure 2.12). Insert changes in the types of movements performed and in the "effort aspect" of movement. (Effort is defined as the qualitative aspects of movement, such as time, force, space, and flow.) Combinations such as running and jumping, as well as moving and stopping to work on specific areas of the body, may also be included. The focus is on quality dance movement within the set task range.

Teaching Tip: You may set tasks like the following: Walk through the room's empty spaces in direct pathways in time with the music; walk and turn, as you move through the spaces in time with the music; walk, turn, and lead with different body parts through the spaces; skip through the spaces in time with the music; add a turn to this skip, as you move through the spaces; create movement phrases in groups of four, with walks and skips; smooth this sequence with short running steps instead of walking.

Figure 2.12   Randomly galloping is an appropriate open movement for this activity.

13. Parts of Speech

Goal: Students experience an interdisciplinary study unit combining physical activity and language arts to enliven parts of speech.

Formation: Open

Procedure: Use the adverb, verb, and preposition for this activity. These words are defined as follows:

adverb—A word used to modify a verb, adjective, or another adverb, such as "quickly, slowly, happily, or sadly"

verb—A word that expresses action, such as "run, jump, slide, or leap"

preposition—A word that shows the relationship of a noun, pronoun, verb, or modifiers in a sentence, such as "on, off, over, under, around, and through"

Make cards large enough so students can read them from 25 yards (see Figure 2.13). Make the adverb cards one color, the verb cards a different color, and the preposition cards another color. Write the parts of speech and the words on the cards. Three students can hold up a card, and the students participating can read and follow the direction that the card indicates. The adverb is *happily*, the verb is *run*, and the preposition is *along* might be a combination that appears in the cards.

Figure 2.13   This game enables students to have fun as well as to make a connection between physical activity and the parts of speech.

Teaching Tip: Change the cards when the students are successfully doing what they describe. This will give the students a variety of action and a hilarious interpretation of some movements. Turn on the music. This is a great way to reinforce the effort qualities of dance.

A List of Adverbs to Help Get Started:

rapidly, calmly, cheerfully, lively, happily, suddenly, teasingly, sneakingly, quietly, loudly, slyly, furtively, forcefully, swiftly, slowly, quickly, foolishly, laughingly, busily, beastly, sternly, stiffly, patiently, playfully, merrily

A List of Verbs to Help Get Started:

jump, sit, run, jog, hop, skip, twirl, leap, gallop, catch, crawl, stumble, pedal, roll, shake, Cha-Cha

A List of Prepositions to Help Get Started:

about, above, across, along, among, around, behind, before, below, beneath, beside, between, beyond, down, through, from, inside, into, near, off, on, out, over, past, toward, under, up

This activity offers a tremendous opportunity for creative movement and dance and for learning these three parts of speech.

To motivate the students, add music—classical music, current music, or instrumental music with a definite beat. A natural follow-up would be for students to add nouns, pronouns, and adjectives to form sentences and to combine sentences to form paragraphs.

14. Run, Stop, Pivot

Goal: Students run, stop, and pivot through the open spaces (see Figure 2.14).

Formation: Open

Procedure: This activity is basic to many of the dances and games we play today. As the name implies, it involves running, stopping, and pivoting through the open spaces. Run, Stop, Pivot can also be done with a partner. The partners are to stay together as if they are guarding one another or dancing with each other. Using partners is also a great way to practice and improve both of these skills simultaneously.

Teaching Tip: With different kinds of music, use the movements to help develop the participants' dance skills to their highest levels. As you plan, remember the progression: Move from locomotors (K-2), to combinations (3-5), to selected dance steps (6-8).

Figure 2.14   Run, Stop, Pivot can improve students' fitness and provide them a foundation for many other dance activities.

15. Talking Drum

Goal: Students move to the beat of the drum or other percussion instrument.

Formation: Open

Procedure: Students follow the talking drum, changing movements according to the speed and intensity of the beats (see Figure 2.15). You can suggest movement changes in directions, levels, pathways, body parts, and so on.

Figure 2.15   Moving to a drumbeat is a great way for students to learn new movements.

Teaching Tip: Using equipment such as balls, hoops, and ropes would be a strong addition to this activity. Tell the students what movement to do, or have a student select the movement to do with your drumbeat. Practice all movements with even and uneven drumbeats.

16. Wall Work

Goal: Students develop strength and flexibility.

Formation: Students are around the walls in your gyms, rooms, and buildings (see Figure 2.16).

Procedure: Use the walls for resistive work and stretching.

Teaching Tip: Dance movements can be done between exercises to raise activity levels and to reinforce or learn dance movements. Follow the progression—locomotors, combinations, selected dance steps.

Figure 2.16   Walls offer a good surface to work on and allow several students to participate at the same time.

SMALL-GROUP ACTIVITIES

As with the large-group activities, the small-group activities assist you in meeting your fitness and dance needs. They have been modified to teach your students fitness and a variety of dance skills.

17. Group Creation

Goal: Students create a dance sequence using the elements you set in the task.

Formation: Open

Procedure: Use this as a culminating activity for the students. Groups of 2 to 10 students create a dance sequence using the elements set in the task (see Figure 2.17).

Teaching Tip: After your students have practiced a number of the dance steps, instruct them to put these movements together in their own creative sequences.

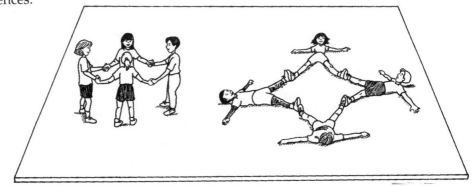

Figure 2.17   These students hold hands and create a new shape from their first formation.

18. Lines and Leaders

Goal: Each student can be a leader to further develop and enhance dance skills.

Formation: Put the class in lines with about 5 feet between each person; the first person faces the head of his or her line (see Figure 2.18).

Figure 2.18   Jumping, sliding, and skipping are locomotor movements your students can use in Lines and Leaders.

Procedure: Everyone gets to be a leader. The student at the front leads dance movements that have already been learned in class. On your signal, everyone rotates forward and the leader goes to the end of the line. The exercises continue. During rotation, everyone jogs in place until the new leader starts the next dance movement.

Teaching Tip: You determine the types of dance movements or have the students select the movements they want to do. This is done with musical accompaniment. Again, follow the locomotor, combination, and selected dance step progression.

19. Partner Over and Under

Goal: Students develop movement skills through changing environments.

Formation: Open

Procedure: One partner moves over, under, around, and through the empty spaces formed by a bridge made by the other partner's body (see Figure 2.19). A variation of this activity is to have movers go from one bridge to another.

Teaching Tip: You suggest changing how, where, and what occurs in a student's movement pattern to raise the quality of the overall movement. All movements in and through space should be dance movements.

Figure 2.19   One student crawls through another student's arched body. This activity can help students adapt their movements to other situations.

20. Small Circles

Goal: Students have an opportunity to develop leadership skills while improving rhythmic skills.

Formation: Circles (see Figure 2.20)

Procedure: Change leaders in the ring periodically to provide variety in the activity and the movements. The leader selects a dance movement to demonstrate; the students in the circle do the dance with rhythmic accompaniment.

Teaching Tip: When working with K-2 students, remember to reinforce locomotor movements; at the 3-5 level, support combinations; and at the 6-8 level, develop the selected dance steps along with everything else.

Figure 2.20   Small circles allow for an intimate environment with less risk for the students.

CIRCUITS

Most readers are probably wondering, "Circuits? In a book on rhythm and dance?" The answer is a definite yes! For instance, in every circuit that you design, there is a good reason to include a rhythms station. The travel from station to station can focus on rhythmic and dance movements. Another way to get rhythm and dance into your circuits is to come to the middle of the teaching area before switching stations and practice rhythmic dance movements. The following examples offer ideas to do what has just been discussed.

21. Circuit 1 (Stations 1-8)

Goal: Students have an opportunity to learn activities that will help them develop and achieve total fitness, and to learn and reinforce a variety of dance skills.

Formation: Stations (see Figure 2.21)

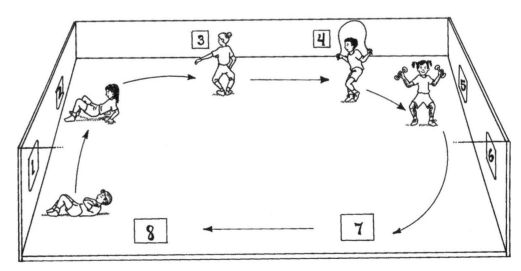

Figure 2.21   Students can do a number of movements at Circuit 1 stations, including abdominal crunches, crab push-ups, and pliés.

Procedure: Instruct students to start walking, jogging, or practicing a dance step, then go to a station when the music changes and do the task posted there. Suggest no more than five people per station; do 1 to 10 repetitions of each exercise, but no more than double the specified number. Instruct students to switch stations when you are ready. (Options: Go to the center of the room for 90 seconds of aerobic dance; practice locomotor or combination movements around the teaching area; practice selected dance steps to the next station). Move around the room clockwise.

Teaching Tip: The rhythmic skills that can be reinforced during this activity are endless. Your choice should be based on both the grade levels and the developmental levels of your students as discussed earlier.

Suggested Moves:

Station 1. Abdominals

Do curl-ups.

Do crunches.

Perform knee-to-chest twists.

Station 2. Arms

Do crab push-ups.

Do pull-ups.

Station 3. Quadriceps

Perform pliés.

In plié position, bounce ball off wall 1 to 20 times.

Station 4. Jump Rope

Use continuous movement forward and backward with varying patterns.

Station 5. Upper Back Rhomboids

With bent knees and hips in straddle position, do flys with weights, 1 to 20 times.

Station 6. Chest

Lie on bench or floor; do flys with weights, 1 to 20 times.

Station 7. Aerobic Dance Steps

Gallop between markers.

Slide between markers.

Skip between markers.

Station 8. Line Touch

Run back and forth between the lines touching the line with the hand each time, 1 to 20 times. (Variations: Use a different locomotor each time, use different combinations, or different dance steps.)

22. Circuit 2 (Stations 1-8)

Goal: Students have an opportunity to learn activities that will help them develop and achieve total fitness, and to learn and reinforce a variety of dance skills.

Formation: Stations (see Figure 2.22)

Procedure: Instruct students to start walking, jogging, or practicing a dance step, then on a signal, go to a station and do the activity. Suggest no more than five people per station. Switch stations on the signal; go to the center for 90 seconds of aerobic dance between stations. Move around the room clockwise.

Teaching Tip: As with the previous circuit, many opportunities exist to develop and reinforce the basic rhythmic and dance movements. At the K-2 level, focus on the locomotors, at the 3-5 level emphasize the combinations, and at the 6-8 level develop the selected dance steps and review all that has preceded. By following this progression you will support your students' developmental needs.

Figure 2.22   Circuit 2 stations like these give students the chance to work on flexibility, upper body strength, and cardiovascular fitness.

Suggested Moves:

Station 1. Shuttle Station

Move between the markers and touch an imaginary line between them.

Move forward, backward, sideward, turning and changing patterns like the skip, gallop, and Schottische. Focus on rhythmic elements at the appropriate level.

Repeat the sequences until the signal; then move to the next station. (Special note: Movement to the next station can include any of the rhythmic movements or inviting everyone to the center to practice any movements that you choose.)

Station 2. Flexibility—Hip Girdle Stretching

Select your own stretch.

Do a slow, gentle, static stretch.

Move to the next station on signal.

Station 3. Crabwalk

Crabwalk between markers.

First go forward, then backward, then sideward.

Repeat until the next signal; then move to the next station.

Station 4. Jump and Reach

Practice vertical jump, over and over.

Practice standing long jump repeatedly, for distance.

Move to the next station on signal.

Station 5. Sit-Ups

Use slow, continuous movement.

Do as many as possible; move to the next station on signal.

Station 6. Flexibility—Shoulder Girdle Stretching

Select your own stretch.

Do a slow, gentle, static stretch.

Move to the next station on signal.

Station 7. Walk on All Fours

Walk on all fours back and forth between the markers.

First go forward, then backward, then sideward.

Repeat until the next signal; then move to the next station.

Station 8. Rope Jumping

Turn the rope continuously until the next signal; use a variety of turns and jumps.

23. Countdown

Goal: Students have an opportunity to learn activities that will help them develop and achieve total fitness, and to learn and reinforce a variety of dance skills.

Formation: Stations (see Figure 2.23)

Procedure: Instruct students to start walking, jogging, or practicing a dance step around the outside of the room or the markers. On signal, students work their way from the "jog five laps" sign down to the "walk one lap" sign. They should not do more than twice the suggested number of repetitions. Students work at their own pace.

Teaching Tip: Since this activity calls for the students to jog in between stations, this is an opportunity for them to practice locomotors, combinations, or selected dance steps, according to where they are developmentally. In your

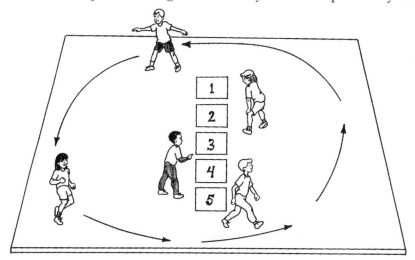

Figure 2.23   An activity set up in different stations can hold your students' attention as well as enhance their physical fitness.

selection of rhythmic movements, remember that the focus is primarily on locomotors at the K-2 level, combinations at the 3-5 level, and selected dance steps at the 6-8 level.

Suggested Moves:

Jog one lap or do aerobic dance 1 minute.

Jump rope forward 1 to 30 times.

Jump rope backward 1 to 30 times.

Jog two laps or do aerobic dance 2 minutes.

Balance standing scale, each leg 15 seconds.

Do mule kicks, 1 to 15 times.

Jog three laps or do aerobic dance 3 minutes.

Do a long sit with single-leg lifts, 1 to 10 times for each leg.

Sit and reach for your toes, 1 to 10 times for each leg.

Jog four laps or do aerobic dance 4 minutes.

Do push-ups, 1 to 10 times.

Do crab push-ups, 1 to 10 times.

Jog five laps or do aerobic dance 5 minutes.

Do crunches, 1 to 10 times.

Do knee-to-chest twists, 1 to 10 times on each side.

When selecting the content for the next two activities, use the same considerations as in previous activities. The grade levels and developmental levels of your students determine the appropriate rhythmic and dance elements to include at each station.

24. Four Corner Rhythms

Goal: Students have an opportunity to learn activities that will help them develop and achieve total fitness, and to learn and reinforce a variety of dance skills.

Formation: Stations

Procedure: In each corner of the teaching area is a task card giving directions to the next corner (see Figure 2.24). Use music to stress the rhythmic performance

Figure 2.24   While some students read their card for instructions, others use a sliding movement to get to the next station.

of the movements. On your signal, the students go to one of the four corners of the teaching area, with no more than 10 students per corner. When the music starts, they move to the next corner numerically, traveling counterclockwise around the teaching area. They do the activities at level "a" the first time around, level "b" the second time, and level "c" the third time. For example: Slide from corner 1 to corner 2, skip to corner 3, gallop to corner 4, and run and turn to corner 1. When you get back to your original corner, drop down to level "b" and move around the room doing the activities listed for level "b." Continue the activity until you decide it is time to stop.

Teaching Tip: A variation of this is to have students work with a piece of equipment while moving around the room. Balls, ropes, and hoops can accompany these movements. Now invent your own courses.

Suggested Moves:

Corner 1	**Corner 3**
a. Slide	a. Gallop
b. Polka	b. Schottische
c. Run and turn	c. Skip and turn
Corner 2	**Corner 4**
a. Skip	a. Run
b. Grapevine	b. Run and leap
c. Two-step	c. Schottische and turn

25. Obstacle Courses

Goal: Students have an opportunity to learn activities that will help them develop and achieve total fitness, and to learn and reinforce a variety of dance skills.

Formation: Stations

Procedure: Use equipment to set up obstacle courses for students to negotiate. When setting up a course, be sure all components of fitness are being developed. The equipment arrangement should provide students with the opportunity to climb and to use both their upper and lower bodies (see Figure 2.25).

Figure 2.25   An Obstacle Course can challenge students' coordination and strength as well as liven up their class period.

While traveling between obstacles, the students are to use the rhythmic dance movements described in chapter 1 as appropriate to their developmental levels.

Teaching Tip: The focus on rhythmic movements between obstacles is the element that makes this obstacle course different from others.

26. Rhythms Circuit

Goal: Students have an opportunity to learn activities that will help them develop and achieve total fitness, and to learn and reinforce a variety of dance skills.

Formation: Stations (see Figure 2.26)

Procedure: Instruct students to go to the activity area of their choice and start walking, jogging, or practicing dance steps. On your cue, students go to any station and do the rhythmic movement activity on the task card at that station. Rotate to the next station every 1 to 1-1/2 minutes. Suggest no more than five to eight students per station. Switch stations on signal. Move in a clockwise direction.

Teaching Tips—Options: Go to the center of the room and do aerobic dance for 90 seconds; do this activity with equipment at the station; have the student carry the equipment from station to station and perform the task.

Figure 2.26   Rhythmic movements abound in the Rhythms Circuit.

Suggested Moves:

1   Skipping (Walk-Hop)

Skip in the designated area; change directions and stay with the music. Skipping can be done forward, backward, and sideward.

2   Galloping (Walk-Leap)

Gallop in the designated area. Cover the entire area, and remember that galloping can be done forward and backward.

3   Sliding (Walk-Leap)

Slide in the designated area. Let the left foot then the right foot lead the slide sideward.

4   Polka (Slide and Skip or Gallop and Skip)

Practice polka step in the designated area. Pretend to use or use a ball to dribble while practicing this step. Find a partner to act as a guard while dribbling and practicing polka step.

5   Schottische (Walk, Walk, Walk, Hop)

Practice Schottische step forward, backward, and sideward. Include 180-degree and 360-degree turns in the sequence. Practice run, run, run, shoot sequence with or without a ball.

6   Running

Run through the designated area, changing directions, stopping, and pivoting with or without equipment. Find a partner to act as a guard or to begin the process of partnering in dance.

GAMES

There is a strong attraction for us to learn in a gamelike situation. The games in this section are exciting yet low intensity and nonthreatening. Students can learn how to get themselves fit and learn dance skills at the same time.

27. Broken Heart

Goal: Students have an opportunity to learn activities that will help them develop and achieve total fitness, and to learn and reinforce a variety of dance skills.

Formation: Open

Procedure: Give four or more players heart-shaped beanbags, or some other object, to pass to other players while you play music (see Figure 2.27). The

Figure 2.27   Broken Heart provides a natural time to introduce cardiovascular fitness concepts to your students.

students with beanbags try to get rid of them by passing them to those without beanbags (the beanbag or object is a "hot potato" in a sense). Instruct the class to use a set dance movement to travel anywhere in the designated area while the music plays. When you stop the music, all students holding beanbags go to the "Broken Heart" area, and the rest play the game again. The students in the Broken Heart area practice rhythmic dance steps that you select until the next group comes. Thus, the first group returns to the game without having been inactive. This activity continues as long as you want to play the game.

Teaching Tip: Those who are in the Broken Heart area can do flexibility exercises, strength development exercises, rhythmic and dance movements, or whatever you choose until they return to the game.

28. Veins and Arteries

Goal: Students have an opportunity to learn activities that will help them develop and achieve total fitness, and to learn and reinforce a variety of dance skills.

Formation: Following the lines on the floor (see Figure 2.28)

Procedure: This game is similar to Broken Heart with one change. Instruct players to travel only on the lines in the gym. When the music stops, the player holding the object must go to the heart attack area. These players return to the game when the next group enters the area. Players cannot pass others, but can turn around and head the other direction. As with Broken Heart, this game offers an opportunity to discuss components of cardiovascular fitness.

Teaching Tip: In Broken Heart and Veins and Arteries, have students work on rhythmic and dance movements, such as skipping, galloping, sliding, running, and doing the polka with the music.

Figure 2.28 Students must follow the lines on the floor, but they still enjoy fun and fitness.

SUMMARY

Large-group, small-group, circuits, and games—what is your choice? A myriad of opportunities have been opened for your use. These rhythmic activities are for you to use, enjoy, and modify for your special needs. Provide your students with opportunities to modify them and create their own versions. Watch motivation rise.

CHAPTER 3

RHYTHMIC AEROBICS AND DANCE

Aerobics has been and always will be a great medium to develop personal fitness. The more dances and dance steps in a person's repertoire, the more possibilities there are to add variety and excitement to the aerobic and dance program.

This chapter will expand and enhance your base of information immeasurably for your future programs. It includes guidelines and tips for quality aerobics with selected warm-up and cool-down exercise descriptions. These are followed by both low-impact and high-impact sample workouts, and eight routines in a sample workout. The chapter closes with suggestions for creating your own routines and 10 sample aerobic routines for you to try, modify, and use in your classes.

Don't neglect this dimension of your dance program. Aerobics and dance movements may well be the ingredients that will open up the entire dance component in your classes.

TIPS FOR QUALITY AEROBICS

The following guidelines will help you provide quality programs for your students. Try to incorporate as many into your classes as you can.

- Keep the class running smoothly.
- Monitor pulse rates regularly.
- Train adequately in first aid and CPR.
- Advise students on appropriate footwear and clothing.
- Screen students for physical abnormalities.
- Indicate to students when high-impact and low-impact aerobics are being used.

How to Get a Resting Heart Rate

After you wake up in the morning, while still lying in bed, count your pulse for a full minute at either the carotid or radial arteries. Simply place your index and middle fingers on the skin above the artery with enough pressure to feel a heartbeat and start counting for a full minute. This number is your resting heart rate.

How to Calculate Your Target Heart Rate Zone

The Karvonen formula has become a standard in the exercise industry for calculating target heart rate zones. The intensity at which you exercise can be modified to accommodate individual fitness levels. Beginners should multiply heart rate reserve by .40, intermediate exercisers by .50, and advanced students by .60 to .80. The formula is as follows:

1. 220 – Age = Estimated maximal heart rate
2. Maximal heart rate – Resting heart rate = Heart rate reserve
3. Heart rate reserve × 0.40 = _____ + Resting heart rate = Target heart rate
4. Target heart rate – 10 = Lower end of target zone
5. Target heart rate + 10 = Higher end of target zone

Four Criteria to Make Movements Aerobic

Aerobic benefits occur whenever the following four criteria are met:

- Continuous movement without stopping
- 12 to 15 minutes, up to 60 minutes
- Three to five times a week
- 60% to 80% target heart rate

Low-impact aerobics are characterized by movements (in which one foot stays in contact with the floor) which are less stressful on the joints. During high-impact aerobics both feet will have no contact with the floor at various times. Having the option of high- and low-impact aerobics will allow students and teachers to decide which level is best for a particular workout.

Three Parts of an Aerobic Routine

A balanced aerobic workout needs three parts.

1. Warm-up—A balanced combination of static stretching and rhythmic limbering exercises that warms the muscle core; should be engaged in after walking briskly in place.

2. Aerobics—At least 20 to 30 minutes of rhythmic movement consisting of leg, arm, chest, and shoulder work; goal is to raise the heart rate to improve cardiovascular respiration. First select low-impact movements and dance steps and gradually move to high-impact and more complex steps.

3. Cool-down—A balanced combination of stretching and breathing that reduces heart rate and muscle soreness.

Exercise Guidelines

When you develop aerobic routines, you should consider a number of factors to create a sound program. Keep in mind the following points:

- Get a resting pulse rate before starting session.
- Start slowly; gradually increase the number of minutes of continuous (nonstop) movement.
- Encourage participants to walk 5 to 15 minutes prior to session as an initial warm-up.
- It's the choice of exercises and the way you do them that makes the workout effective, productive, and fun.
- Slow, gentle stretches (static) are much better than fast, violent movements (ballistic).
- Knees and elbows should not be locked, or hyperextended, while exercising.
- Squats should not exceed 90 degrees.
- Sit-ups should be executed in a curling motion with bent knees and the lower back flat on the floor. Curl only about 40 degrees from the floor.
- Double-leg lifts are not to be done at any time.

- Students should be reminded to pull their stomachs in and buttocks under while exercising ("dining room in and sitting room under" or "suck and tuck").

- Routines should develop harmony in movements, teach fine balance, coordination, grace, and control.

- Workouts should include a gradual warm-up, an aerobic period, and a gradual cool-down.

- The cool-down should be done slowly and with adequate stretching to avoid muscle soreness.

- The exercise length should be 40 to 60 minutes: 10- to 15-minute warm-up, 15 to 20 minutes of exercise at one's target heart rate, 10- to 15-minute cool-down (minimum).

- Indicate whether the routine is low or high impact.

SELECTED WARM-UP AND COOL-DOWN EXERCISE DESCRIPTIONS

Virtually every area of the body is included in this section, with at least one exercise for your routines. Include all the body parts for warming up, using one choice for each body part. Use music for these exercises, to keep the beat while walking or marching and to offer a rhythmic experience by grouping movements in counts of eight.

Head and Neck

Head and neck exercises will improve circulation and reduce stress and tension. Use slow, soothing music.

Neck extension will improve flexibility and range of motion. Sit up comfortably. Bend the head forward gently toward the chest, then straighten back up to the vertical position, returning to the starting position, and slowly rotate the head to the left. Return to starting position and slowly rotate the head to the right. Return to starting position. The head may also be tilted slowly and comfortably to the left and the right. Do not lay the head backward or move backward from side to side.

Face stretches relieve muscle tension in the face. Raise the eyebrows and open the eyes as wide as possible. At the same time, open the mouth, stretch the muscles around the chin and nose, and stick the tongue out. Hold this stretch 5 to 10 seconds.

Shoulder

Shoulder exercises are designed to improve flexibility and upper body strength and to relax the muscles at the base of the neck. Use slow music.

The **shoulder shrug** is for the upper back; it tones the shoulders and relaxes the muscles at the base of the neck. Lift the shoulders up and then relax them.

Touch shoulders is to increase the flexibility of the shoulders and elbows and to tone the upper arms. It can be done in a seated position. Touch the shoulders with the hands, extend the arms straight out with the fists closed, and bring the arms back to the starting position.

Figure 3.1   Shoulder stretch 1.

Shoulder stretch 1 is for shoulder flexibility. Interlace the fingers above the head. Now, with the palms facing upward, push the arms slightly back and up (see Figure 3.1). Hold this stretch for 15 seconds. Feel the stretch on the upper arms, shoulders, and upper back. This is great for slumping shoulders.

Shoulder stretch 2 is to stretch the triceps and the tops of the shoulders. With the arms overhead, hold the elbow of one arm with the hand of the other arm. Gently pull the elbow behind the head, creating a stretch. Do this slowly, and hold it for 15 seconds. This can be done while walking.

Shoulder stretch 3 is to stretch the shoulders and upper back. Gently pull the elbow across the chest toward the opposite shoulder. Hold this stretch for 10 seconds.

Shoulder stretch 4 is to stretch the arms, the sides of the body, and the shoulders. With the arms extended overhead, hold the outside of the left hand with the right hand, and pull the left arm to the right side. Keep the arms as straight and comfortable as possible. Hold this for 15 seconds on each side.

Arm

Arm exercises include muscles of the upper torso, biceps, triceps, forearms, hands, and wrists. They increase strength and range of motion and improve flexibility.

Arm circles are to strengthen the shoulders and upper back. Sit or stand erect with the arms at the sides, elbows straight, and head high. Rotate the arms from the shoulders in small to large circles, always keeping the arms slightly flexed.

Arm curls are to strengthen biceps and forearms. Use a weighted object, such as a book or a can of vegetables, not more than 5 pounds. Sit or stand erect with the arms at the sides, palms facing up, holding the weighted object. Bend the arm, raising the weight. Lower it.

Arm extensions are to tone the triceps muscle in the back of the arm. Sit or stand erect with the arms at the sides, palms facing up. Holding a weighted object of less than 5 pounds, extend the arm overhead. Slowly bend the arm until the weight is behind the head. Slowly extend the arm to its original position. The arm curl and arm extension can be done separately or together, alternating arms.

Elbow stretch 1 is to strengthen biceps. Alternate flexion and extension of the elbow joints.

Elbow stretch 2 is to stretch the chest and upper arms. Stretch the arms behind the back with fingers interlaced behind the back. Slowly turn the elbows inward while straightening the arms.

Forearm stretches are done while standing erect. With the palms of the hands flat, the thumbs to the outside, and the fingers pointed backward, slowly lean the arm back to stretch the forearm. Be sure to keep the palms flat.

Hand rotation is to maintain wrist flexibility and range of motion. Grasp the right wrist with the left hand. Keep the right palm facing down. Slowly rotate the hand five times clockwise, then counterclockwise.

Front of Legs

Because the quadriceps represent the largest muscle group in the body, they are used constantly and therefore need to be stretched for less chance of injury.

Quad stretches are usually done against the wall after walking or running. Grasp the ankle with the opposite hand and pull the leg up, attempting to pull the sole of the foot toward the buttocks. Do not lean forward. Hold this for 6 to 10 seconds. Tightness should be felt in the front of the thigh. Go only to the point of tightness; do not push it. Repeat with the other leg.

Back of Legs

Exercising the hamstrings will help the muscle balance between the front and back of the legs and help avoid knee injury.

Trunk bending starts in a sitting position with legs slightly bent and the toes pointed until you feel tightness in the back of the legs. Hold it for 3 seconds. Relax. Gradually work toward the toes.

Trunk bending variation helps reduce some of the stress if the back hurts when bending. Lie on the back, feet flat on the floor near the hips. Bring one leg toward the face. Grasp the lower leg and pull it toward the chest until there is tightness behind the leg. Relax.

Back of Legs

Strengthening the gastrocnemius will lessen chances of knee injury.

Achilles stretch uses the stride position with one leg in front of the other and the toes near a wall. The front knee is bent, and the hands are on the wall (see Figure 3.2). The back leg is straight with the heel flat on the floor. Lean toward the front knee, keeping the back foot and heel flat. Hold this for 6 to 10 seconds. Relax. Repeat with the other leg. If tightness does not occur in the calf during this exercise, the hips may not be pushed enough toward the wall, or the heel may be coming off the floor.

Calf raise is used to strengthen the lower leg and ankle. Stand erect with the hands on the hips or on the back of a chair for balance. Spread the feet 6 to 12 inches apart. Slowly raise the body up on the toes, lifting the heels. Return to the starting position. Repeat 10 to 15 times.

Figure 3.2   Achilles stretch.

Groin

The groin stretch will improve flexibility and allow the legs a larger range of motion.

Spread groin stretch starts in a sitting position with the legs spread apart. Place the hands on the inside of the leg, eventually attempting to reach the inside of the ankles. Bend forward from the hips keeping the knees flat. Hold as soon as there is tightness on the inside of the legs. Relax. Repeat. Think of stretching from the head down; this allows for a total stretch, not just a waist bend.

Ankles

Ankle and foot exercises prepare the feet to support the body, especially with sudden changes in direction.

Ankle and foot circles will improve flexibility and range of motion in the ankles. While sitting, cross the right leg over the left knee; rotate the foot slowly, making large, complete circles. Do 10 rotations to the right; then 10 to the left on each foot.

Chest and Trunk

Chest and trunk exercises are designed to stretch the chest cavity for better ventilation, to develop the upper body, and to maintain muscle tone.

Knee push-ups are very good for upper body development and maintaining muscle tone. Start on the hands and knees with the hands parallel to each other, slightly more than shoulder-width apart. The wider the hands are, the more work for the pectoral muscles.

Chain breaker begins standing with the arms raised to shoulder level in front of the chest. The elbows should be out and the palms down, parallel to the floor. Straighten the elbows and reach back with the hands, palms facing forward. Do not allow the shoulders or the arms to drop below shoulder level.

SELECTED EXERCISE COMPONENTS FOR AEROBICS AND DANCE ROUTINES

In choosing the exercise selections for your warm-up and cool-down routines, select exercises that cover the major muscle groups which are biceps, triceps, quadriceps, gastrocnemius, hamstrings, pectorals, deltoids, and abdominals. The use of 4/4 tempo music offers the student an opportunity for rhythmic movement efficiency and ease. The following lists are suggested movements for three parts of an aerobic workout.

1. Warm-up movements
   - Walk and Jog
   - Head-rolls, bends, isolations
   - Shoulder-rolls, forward, back, up and down
   - Trunk twists and bends
   - Arm circles
   - Wrists
   - Hips
   - Rib cage shift
   - Knee lifts
   - Pliés (toes slightly out, back straight, bend knees to 45 degrees and back up to normal position)
   - Lunges
   - Releves (same position as a plié, move up on toes and back to resting position)

- Straddle sit
- Cat stretch (on hands and knees, raise and lower back)
- Alternate Toe Touch
- William's flexion exercises (on back, lower back flat on floor, pull one knee at a time to the chest, and then both knees)
- Push-ups
- Sit-ups
- Hip raiser–crab position

2. Aerobic movement suggestions
   - Grapevines
   - Charleston
   - Pendulum Swings
   - Heel touch in front
   - Jump kicks
   - Walk circles
   - Gallops
   - Polka Step
   - Cha-Cha
   - Step-hop circling
   - Forward and backward jumping
   - Jazz circles
   - Lindy (single, double, triple)
   - Slides

3. Cool-down movement suggestions
   - Walking or jogging (2 to 5 minutes)
   - Calf stretches
   - Straddle sits
   - Cat stretches
   - William's flexion
   - Stretch body
   - Relaxing
   - Walking or jogging remainder of song

LOW-IMPACT SAMPLE WORKOUT

Note: At least one foot remains on the floor at all times.

1. Warm-up (10 to 15 minutes)
   - Walking or marching
   - Shoulder shrugs

- Arm extensions
- Quad stretches
- Trunk bending
- Spread groin stretches
- Ankle and foot circles

2. Aerobic period (15 to 20 minutes at target heart rate)

- Walk and jog around room or designated area.
- Grapevine four times in each direction, right to left.
- Charleston eight times, four beginning with left foot and four beginning with right foot.
- Heel touch in front by lifting right heel and touching with left hand.
- Walk circles, four to the right (clockwise) and four to the left (counterclockwise).
- Repeat for the duration of this period, keeping it simple so the students can remember and be successful.

3. Cool-down (10 to 15 minutes)

- Walking or jogging 2 to 5 minutes
- Calf stretches
- Straddle sits with one leg bent in toward the body
- Cat stretches

HIGH-IMPACT SAMPLE WORKOUT

Note: Both feet may leave the floor.

1. Warm-up (10 to 15 minutes)

- Walking and jogging
- Head rolls
- Shoulder rolls
- Arm circles
- Quad stretches
- Trunk rotations
- Achilles stretches

2. Aerobic period (15 to 20 minutes)

- Jog around room or designated area.
- Step-hop circling, counterclockwise four times and clockwise four times.
- Jump forward and backward.
- Slides, four to the right and four to the left.
- Polka step for 16 counts.

3. Cool-down (10 to 15 minutes)

- Walking 2 to 5 minutes

- William's flexion series
- Straddle sits with one leg pulled in toward the body
- Cat stretches

LIST OF EIGHT ROUTINES WITHIN A SAMPLE WORKOUT

Get a resting pulse rate before starting session. Encourage participants to walk 5 to 15 minutes prior to session as an initial warm-up. Modify movements to be low or high impact as necessary to best fit students' endurance levels and/or personal requirements.

Warm-Up Routine

Counts and Steps:

PART A:

1-8—Shoulder stretches, four times

1-8—Alternate arm reach across body, four times

1-8—Alternate arm reach to opposite knee, four times

PART B:

1-8—Shoulder shrug up and down, four times

1-8—Shoulder shrug forward and backward, four times

1-8—Arm circles forward, four times

1-8—Arm circles backward, four times

PART C:

1-8—Trunk rotations, four times each way

1-8—Forward lunge and touch floor, two times with each foot in front

1-8—Shoulder stretch 2, four times

1-8—Shoulder stretch 3, four times

PART D:

1-8—Push-pull with elbows high and hands stretching, four times

1-8—Side bends, four times each side

1-8—Ankle and foot circling, four times each way

1-8—Arm circles in front of body, bending low and reaching high, four times each way

Aerobic Exercise Routine 1

Counts and Steps:

PART A:

1-16—Walk or jog in place, lifting knees high and moving arms, 16 counts.

1-8—Lunge forward, dip (hands go down to the floor and then stretch to the floor) and dive, two times with each foot in front.

1-8—Plié, four times.

PART B:

1-8—Lunge to sides, dip and dive, two times to each side.

1-16—Push-pull forward eight and backward eight, two times with the arms.

1-8—Skip to right four times, back to left four times.

PART C:

1-16—Turn to the right side while facing front and bend, four times each to the right and left sides.

1-8—Arm circles while walking in place, four times forward and backward; always have arms slightly bent.

PART D:

1-16—Step-kicks or knee lifts.

PART E:

1-32—Gallop to right, back to left, and then to center, four times.

PART F:

1-16—Twist to right, then full turn to left, four times.

1-16—Plié, four times.

PART G:

1-8—Alternate arm circles while walking in place, four times forward and four times backward; arms slightly bent.

1-8—Breaststroke arm movements while walking in place, eight times.

PART H:

1-16—Walk to right, back to left, and then to center with arms moving and knees up high; alternate right and left, two times.

1-16—Standing straddle stretch to floor, four times; maintain a flat back and bend knees slightly.

Note: Strive to reach the target heart rate zone during this aerobic routine. The next four routines can be either low or high impact depending on your needs. Any of the routines may be modified from high impact to low impact or vice versa. Simply remember what designates a high- and low-impact activity.

Aerobic Exercise Routine 2—Freedom Hop

Music: Wham! *Freedom*, Columbia Records, 44-05238 Long Mix. xss 174437.

Formation: Lines

Counts and Steps:

PART A:

1-32—Step right, step left, step right and kick left forward; step left, step right, step left and kick right backward. Repeat eight times with a quarter turn after each set.

PART B:

1-16—Chassé step; step right foot, left foot, right foot and place left foot behind right foot and rock back; step left foot, right foot, left foot and place right foot behind left foot and rock back. Repeat four times.

1-16—Step-hop back step; step right on right foot and hop on right foot. Step left foot behind right foot. Step left on left foot and hop on left foot. Step right foot behind left foot. Repeat four times.

PART C:

1-16—Do four complete Cha-Cha steps, counting 1, 2, 3-and-4; 5, 6, 7-and-8.

1-16—Repeat the steps for counts 1 to 16 in Part B.

PART D:

1-32—Repeat the steps for counts 1 to 32 in Part A.

PART E:

1-16—Repeat the steps for first set of counts 1 to 16 in Part B.

1-16—Repeat the steps for first set of counts 1 to 16 in Part C.

PART F:

1-16—March four steps forward and four steps backward, turning to the right a quarter turn until back to the front; repeat marching to the left.

1-16—Repeat the steps for first set of counts 1 to 16 in Part B.

1-16—Repeat the steps for second set of counts 1 to 16 in Part B to the end of music.

Aerobic Exercise Routine 3—Hopscotch Fun

Music: Billy Joel, "Tell Her About It, " on *An Innocent Man*, Columbia Records CBS, QC 38837.

Formation: Lines

Counts and Steps:

PART A:

1-16—Hopscotch step, eight times.

1-16—Grapevine to the right four steps, then to the left four steps.

PART B:

1-16—Slide right as in the Gallop; then to the left.

1-16—Pull-downs; arms lifted above the head; pull the arms down as the knees are lifted; begin with the right, and alternate right and left, eight times.

Repeat the dance.

Check heart rate.

Aerobic Exercise Routine 4—Kicking Fun

Music: Mike Post, "The A-Team Theme," on *Album*, RCA AFL1-5415 previously released on AFL1-5183. Mike Post, "Footloose," on *Album*, RCA AFL1-5415 previously released on AFL1-5183.

Formation: Lines, and when learned, try a circle.

Counts and Steps:

PART A:

1-8—Step-kick; step-kick beginning on right foot, then on left foot; alternate four times.

1-8—Jumping jacks, four times.

PART B:

1-16—Step behind, step-kick with three kicks; alternate right left, right, then left, four times.

1-16—Rocking horse side-to-side, eight times.

Repeat the dance.

Aerobic Exercise Routine 5—Rocking Horse

Music: Elvis Presley, "Good Luck Charm," on Vol. 2 of *20 Greatest Hits*, RCA International, INTS 5116 (NL43343) Cassette INTK 5116.
Formation: Lines

Counts and Steps:

PART A:

1-16—Rocking horse; rock forward on right leg and back on left leg, or forward on left leg and back on right leg, eight times.

1-16—Step, turn around, step together to the right, then to the left, four times.

PART B:

1-16—Pivot step to the right, make a quarter turn on each pivot; return to the front. Then pivot step to the left, make a quarter turn on each pivot; return to the front.

1-8—Click heels together, four times for eight counts.

Repeat the dance.

Aerobic Exercise Routine 6—Get Away

Music: Bobby Brown, "Get Away," MCA Records, MCACS 54511.

Counts and Steps:

PART A:

1-16—Step-close-step (counts 1-and-2) going side-to-side, eight times.

1-16—Step-hops while circling, eight step-hops.

PART B:

1-16—Grapevine right and left, two times.

1-16—Ankle rotations, eight times with each foot.

PART C:

1-16—Rock forward and rock backward, four times each way.

1-16—Arm circles in front of body, bending low and reaching high with arms bent, four times each way.

PART D:

1-16—Lunge forward, big arm circles and pull with arms bent, eight times with each foot in front.

1-16—Modified hurdle stretch, four times each side with right foot and leg bent in toward other leg.

PART E:

1-16—Curls at own pace for 16 counts, knees bent and arms crossed.

1-16—Push-ups, 16 counts at own pace.

Cool-Down and Stretch Routine

Music: Slow 4/4 time.

Counts and Steps:

1-8—Kneeling press and stretch, flex and extend under body, four times.

1-8—Knee-to-chest pull, four times each side, lying on back.

1-8—Both-knees-to-chest pull, four times.

1-8—Total body stretch, one or two times with a static, no-bounce stretch.

1-32—Standing and breathing. Do push-pull or inhaling and exhaling, eight counts at a time. Stress relaxing the body and maintaining good posture.

Check heart rate. Walk for rest of time (or longer, if heart rate is still high).

CREATING RHYTHMIC AEROBIC ROUTINES AND DANCES

This section can provide every class the opportunity to develop creativity and performance as a culminating activity for its programs. Creating a dance fulfills a desire for something new. This can decrease boredom and improve the quality of movement.

When teaching youth, stay up to date by keeping the music youthful, vital. Invite students to contribute, and they will feel important if you use their music, suggestions, or ideas.

There are three basic parts to this section. The first part is "reading the music" or learning to listen. It explains how to coordinate the music with the routine when choreographing a piece. The second part includes sample routines and dances choreographed to popular music. These are to assist you in getting ideas flowing for the development of your routines. This will lead to the third part, which includes a unique activity called "create-a-dance" cards. With this you are one step closer to creating your own rhythmic aerobic routines and dances.

Reading the Music

Music makes the movement activities appealing and fun. The first step is music selection. Once you have music that will appeal to your group, the next step is a process that is very primitive. Listen to the music with paper and pencil in hand, and make a mark on the sheet for each beat:

```
////
////
////
////
////
////
////
////
```

Whenever the music changes, draw a line under the marks to indicate the change, and continue to mark the beats. Then go back and write in the margin what is happening in the music where the changes are indicated. You may add the first few words of the song to use as a cue for teaching it.

When you have written all the cue words, divide the song into its parts and determine the number of beats that each part gets. Here is the music for Jingle Bells:

Counts	1	2	3	4		5	6	7	8
	/	/	/	/		/	/	/	/
	Jin	gle	Bells			Jin	gle	Bells	

Counts	1	2	3	4		5	6	7	8
	/	/	/	/		/	/	/	/
	Jin	gle	All	the		Way . . .			

This represents the first 16 counts. This is the count that you use to determine what dance step or exercise would fit the music.

For example,

Introduction	8 counts
Verse A	32 counts
Verse B	32 counts
Chorus	32 counts
Chorus	32 counts

Now you are ready to add the steps that will create the dance.

Introduction	8 counts	—Alternate right foot, then left foot, and step right foot, step left foot, step right foot, step left foot.
Verse A	32 counts	—Cha-Cha forward and backward, repeat four times.
Verse B	32 counts	—Cross Cha-Cha; cross right foot over left foot and reverse, repeat four times.
Chorus	32 counts	—Slide right and slide left, four times.
Chorus	32 counts	—Slide left and slide right, four times.

Now that you have outlined the routine and selected steps, you are ready to teach it. This is an example of the whole process.

SAMPLE AEROBIC AND DANCE CREATIONS 1-10

The following dances were created using this format and method. The selections are varied with low- and high-impact routines. As you practice the dances, review the process to develop these dances. You will see how easy it is to create them, and you will become more proficient at developing them yourself.

List of Sample Aerobic Dance Routines

1. All I Need Is a Miracle

Music: Mike and the Mechanics, "All I Need Is a Miracle," Atlantic Records, CS 81908.

Formation: Circle or lines; directions are the same for boys and girls.

Counts and Steps:

PART A:

1-4—Sunshine up and down; move hands and arms up and down in a spread-open fashion to imitate the sun's rays.

5-8—Extend left heel and right heel; alternate by placing the heel to the front.

1-8—Hustle right; begin with feet together. Step to the side on the right foot, step behind the right foot with the left foot; step to the side on the right foot, kick with the left foot. Turn around and hustle left and turn around.

1-8—Knee lifts, eight times.

1-8—Step-kick, four times.

PART B:

1-8—Turn around, four steps in a complete circle.

1-8—Hustle right and turn; hustle left and turn.

1-8—Knee lifts, eight times.

1-8—Step left and lunge left; punch diagonally right and left, alternating to the end of the music.

2. Beach Rock

Music: "I Just Called to Say I Love You," Motown, 1745 MF67090. Change the music as often as possible.

Formation: Line

Counts and Steps:

PART A:

1-16—Hustle step, eight steps forward and eight steps back.

1-16—Grapevine right eight steps, and Grapevine left eight steps.

PART B:

1-16—Repeat the steps for the first set of counts 1 to 16 in Part A.

1-16—Six step-kicks; begin on the right foot.

PART C:

1-8—Two rock-steps, forward and backward.

1-16—Four step-pulls to the right, and four step-pulls to left.

PART D:

1-16—Repeat the steps for the second set of counts 1 to 16 in Part B.

1-16—Four rock-steps, forward and backward.

Repeat the dance.

3. Best Friends

Choreographed by: Carri Riemer, 11; Kelly Meshaw, 13; Evan Overton, 11; and Charlie Smithwick, 13.

Music: Bill Medley and Jennifer Warnes, "I've Had The Time Of My Life," on *Dirty Dancing*, MCA Records, MCAC 42257.

Formation: Partners' directions are for the boys, and the girls do the opposite. Boy faces the girl and holds hands. Boy rolls the girl into his arms, then rolls her out.

Counts and Steps:

PART A:

1-4—Boy faces the girl and holds hands. Chassé together facing each other. Begin with feet together, step right foot, left foot, right foot, and place the left foot behind the right foot, and rock back. Step left foot, right foot, left foot, and place right foot behind left foot, and rock back.

5-8—Boy turns the girl to his right, under his arm.

1-16—Shag step for 16 counts; begin on the left foot, right foot, left foot, right foot, left foot, right foot, rock back on left foot and forward on right foot.

1-4—Repeat the steps for first set of counts 1 to 4.

5-8—Repeat the steps for first set of counts 5 to 8.

PART B:

1-16—Repeat the steps for counts 1 to 16 in Part A.

Repeat the dance.

This dance will be appropriate for any Cha-Cha. Use new music to keep the students interested and challenged. This recommendation was made by the creators.

4. Charleston

Assisted by: Donna Cannon and Linda Horne

Music: Pee Wee Hunt and His Orchestra, "12th Street Rag," Shapiro Bernstein and Jerry Vogel Music, X-6001.

Formation: Lines

Counts and Steps:

PART A:

1-16—Four Charleston steps; begin on left foot.

1-16—Eight circle jogs to the right; eight circle jogs to the left.

PART B:

1-16—Four side lunges; right, left, right, left.

1-16—Eight arm circles from the elbow with both arms.

Repeat the dance.

5. Crazy Cha-Cha

Music: Neil Sedaka, "Calendar Girl," RCA Aldon Music, 447-0575. Neil Sedaka, "Breaking Up Is Hard To Do," RCA Aldon Music, 447-0701. Neil Sedaka, "Next Door To An Angel," RCA Aldon Music, 447-0701.

Any Cha-Cha music

Formation: Facing partners; directions are for the boys, and the girls do the opposite.

Counts and Steps:

PART A:

1-16—Four Cha-Cha steps forward and backward; begin on the left foot.

1-16—Four cross Cha-Cha steps; begin on the left foot.

PART B:

1-16—Four Cha-Cha steps forward and backward; begin on the left foot.

1-4—Four Cha-Cha chassé steps; begin on the left foot.

Repeat the dance.

This dance is very easy to adapt to any music with the count of 1, 2, 1, 2, 3, or 1, 2, cha, cha, cha.

6. German Circle Dance

Music: Any polka music will be good.

Formation: Circle with no partners; stand in a circle facing the center, feet together.

Counts and Steps:

1-4—Step right foot to right side and back together. Step left foot to left side and back together.

5-8—Step right heel forward and back together. Step left heel forward and back together.

1-8—Turn counterclockwise to right and step right foot, step left foot, step right foot, step together step; and step left foot, step right foot, step left foot, step together step.

1-8—One half Grapevine step; step right and put weight on right foot, step left behind right and put weight on left foot. Step right and put weight on right foot, and turn a full circle clockwise until facing the center of circle.

Repeat the dance.

7. Jitterbug Mixer

Assisted by: Carri Riemer, 12, who told me that this would be an easy way to teach the Jitterbug.

This mixer incorporates the Double Lindy step, the three step turn, the Jitterbug Jump, and the sugar-foot turn with partners, before students learn the actual Jitterbug. This mixer made teaching the Jitterbug very simple. Partners face each other, boy on the inside of the circle and the girl on the outside of the circle, two hands joined. These directions are for the boy; girls do the opposite.

Counts and Steps:

1-8—Begin with feet together. Step left foot, right foot behind left foot; step right foot, touch right foot to left foot, step right, making a complete turn. Step right foot, left foot, right foot.

1-4—Double Lindy step, left toe heel, right toe heel, left rock-step backward.

5-8—Jitterbug Jump; jump on both feet to the left, jump on both feet to the right. Each jump is made to the diagonal with the boy and girl jumping in opposite directions, holding hands.

1-8—Repeat the steps for second set of counts 5 to 8.

1-8—Suzie Q Turn; join right hands shoulder level and turn clockwise using the Suzie Q Turn. Place weight on balls of the feet and twist the feet, alternating left foot and right foot. At the same time twist the upper body, hips, and torso. Pull against each other while turning clockwise and shake the other hand in the air as if you were waving. On the completion of the turn, move to the right to face a new partner.

Repeat the dance.

8. Just a Gigolo

Assisted by: Carri Riemer

Music: David Lee Roth, "Just A Gigolo, I Ain't Got Nobody," on *Crazy From The Heat*, Warner Bros. EP, 1-25222.

Formation: Double circle, couples side-by-side holding inside hands, facing clockwise. Boys are on the inside and girls on the outside of the circle. Instructions are for the boys; girls do the opposite.

Counts and Steps:

1-8—Walk four steps forward in the line of direction. Turn around individually, dropping hands. Rejoin hands as they walk backward four steps in the same line of direction.

Reverse directions and walk forward four steps. Turn around individually, dropping hands. Rejoin hands as they walk backward four steps in the same line of direction.

1-8—Step back on left foot, right foot, left foot, and forward on right foot, left foot, and right foot.

1-4—The boy turns four steps to the left to meet a new partner. The girl turns around to the right, in place.

5-8—With new partner repeat the steps for third set of 1 to 8 counts.

Repeat the dance.

9. Mirror Dance

Assisted by: Carri Riemer, 11

Music: Kenny Rogers and Kim Carnes, "Don't Fall in Love with a Dreamer," Capitol Records, LV 51152.

Formation: Boy and girl facing each other. All boys face the same direction, and all girls face the same direction.

Counts and Steps:

PART A:

1-6—Hands are touching at shoulder level as if they are on a mirror. Arm circles to the side; right hand for girl and left hand for the boy, 16 counts.

1-8—Both hands make circles at the same time, eight counts.

1-8—Both hands do the bicycle arms alternating right and left, eight counts.

PART B:

1-16—Four Cha-Cha steps; boy steps forward on left foot, girl steps backward on right foot.

1-16—Four cross Cha-Cha steps; boy crosses left foot over right foot, girl crosses right foot over left foot.

PART C:

1-16—Repeat the steps for first set of counts 1 to 16 in Part B.

1-16—Four Cha-Cha pivot turns; boy steps across the left foot with the right foot and turns away from girl. Girl steps across the right foot with the left foot and turns away from boy.

PART D:

1-16—Four Cha-Cha chassé turns; boy turns on left foot forward first, girl turns forward when on right foot.

1-16—Cha-Cha until the end of the music.

10. Simplicity Shag

Music: The Embers, "I Love Beach Music," Entertainment Enterprises, EEE-1001.

Formation: Girl on boy's right side, holding hands; side-by-side facing front.

Counts and Steps:

PART A:

1-8—Shag step is the same as the Triple Lindy step except, instead of moving side-to-side, the step moves forward and backward. The count is 1 and 2, 3, and 4, 5, 6, adding a quarter turn facing partner.

1-8—Shag step, make a quarter turn facing back, side-by-side.

1-8—Shag step, make a quarter turn facing partner.

1-8—Each partner, Shag to turn in circle.

PART B:

1-32—Shag for 32 counts, facing partners.

Repeat the dance.

CREATE-A-DANCE CARDS: THE "CDC" SYSTEM

The "Create-A-Dance Cards" provide any way to make the creation of rhythmic aerobic routines and dances very simple. They are extremely workable. When the music has been selected and analyzed as described in this chapter, select a card at random. On one side of the card, the dance step will be written. On the other side will be the description of the step and an explanation of how to do the movement. To make sure that you are successful with the step, review the count and practice with the music (see Figure 3.3, a and b). Try the step with the introduction, the verse, the chorus, or an instrumental segment.

Figure 3.3 Sample CDC card.

This procedure will give you thousands of combinations that will enhance a dance or exercise class, and will prevent boredom from taking over in your classes.

Not only can you use dance steps in your creations, but you can use sports steps as well. For example, dribbling a basketball requires good timing and rhythm. By using music to maintain a definite tempo for every bounce, the student creates a pattern that is consistent. The unconscious success will enable the student to transfer this skill to the game. The same principle holds true for the pivot step in basketball, the drop kick in soccer, the punt kick in football, and the one, two, three-step release in bowling. These sports skills and more can be done to music. What better way could you choose to improve a child's timing and rhythm!

This approach to creating your own dances or rhythmic aerobic routines has proven successful and will demonstrate magnificent results. At the same time, you and your students are learning skills beyond just combining moves that work.

Class Management

When working with large numbers, divide the class into small clusters of four, six, or eight students. Write a dance step or exercise on a sheet of paper or a card. Include one dance step or exercise with its definition and description per card. Mix the cards up, and let the students select a card. That movement will be each student's contribution to the routine. In each cluster, have the students decide how many times to do the movement, in what order to arrange the movement, the formation for the routine, and the objective of the routine.

This approach teaches children many aspects of physical skills as well as socialization skills.

Music selection is crucial because music is the instrument used to motivate. Motivation will determine the success of the activity. As you will discover, there are as many combinations as there are clusters. The class can learn each cluster's routine. This activity alone could last for 2 weeks. The students will feel that their contributions were worthwhile, and both you and the students will experience real success.

For example:

Music: Billy Joel's "Uptown Girl" is composed of 4 counts, 8 counts, 16 counts, and so on. It is very simple to count. You have four students in a cluster. Each student has a card.

- Card 1 Knee lifts

- Card 2 Lunge forward

- Card 3 Punch

- Card 4 Jumping Jacks

Arrange these four movements so they will flow smoothly and can be repeated until the end of the music.

Evaluating Student Success

The students' success can be quickly determined by their positive comments as they work on their tasks. Look for cooperation with fellow students and the signs of ownership of their products. You will not only see the affective outcomes, but also the cognitive and the psychomotor outcomes.

The students can demonstrate their routines, teach them to the class, or write them down so you can teach them to other classes. The sky's the limit.

SUMMARY

Rhythmic aerobics and dance are productive methods to motivate students so they can reach their potentials in total fitness. With music as an instrument and conscientious instruction as a guide, the child's development will thrive. This chapter gives you an opportunity to experience the joy of teaching using innovative methods. Take it from here, and you are on your way rhythmically.

CHAPTER 4

LINE DANCES

Line dancing is one of the most fun and exciting forms of dance today. It blends familiar dance steps into a routine that can be adapted to many pieces of music. An appealing feature of line dances is that you can use them with current popular music that children enjoy.

Line dances introduce people to dance in a nonthreatening environment. When music is selected that the dancers like, motivation and success levels go higher. Most of the time, they are partnerless dances done in lines, usually without touching. They can assist with the transition to dances with partners and with skill warm-ups for numerous sports.

Music selection is simple. Use music that you and your students like, and you will always meet success. Some of the dances in this chapter are named for a particular piece of music, but may be danced to other songs. In fact, changing songs and tempos creates interesting results. It pushes your students to new and higher levels of movement achievement and thinking skills.

This chapter contains enough line dances to keep any group of dancers active for quite some time. There are a large number of classics included and some that are more recent. They will add excitement and fun to any class. The dances have been arranged into three groups to assist you in selection. Start with the easiest level dances to ensure success for you and your students. The three levels, beginner, intermediate, and advanced, are determined by the complexity of the formations, steps, and tempo. They correspond approximately to grades K-2, 3-5, and 6-8.

LIST OF LINE DANCES IN THIS CHAPTER

LINE DANCE DESCRIPTIONS FOR THE BEGINNER LEVEL

These line dances will demonstrate traveling in large groups without bumping into others or falling, and changing directions and speeds in response to a variety of rhythms.

Beginner Level Characteristics

Characteristics of learners at this level are expanded into three developmental areas: cognitive, affective, and psychomotor. Awareness of these characteristics assists us in selecting chapter content for planning lessons and units. They offer general guidelines, and in the classroom we will each make our final decisions based on specific needs.

Cognitive

- Recognize that movement concepts are similar in a variety of skills.
- Identify appropriate behaviors in physical activities for participating with others.

Affective

- Enjoy participation alone and with others.
- Appreciate the benefits that accompany cooperation and sharing.
- Show consideration toward others in the physical activity setting.

Psychomotor

- Travel in different ways in a large group without bumping into others or falling.
- Distinguish among straight, curved, and zigzag pathways while traveling in various ways.
- Combine various traveling patterns in time to the music.
- Skip, hop, gallop, and slide using mature motor patterns.

1. Grapevine

Description: The basic step in this dance is the Grapevine step.

Music: "The Heat Is On," MCA Records.

Formation: Lines

Counts and Steps:

1-4—Grapevine right foot, left foot, right foot, and touch left foot.

5-8—Grapevine left foot, right foot, left foot, and touch right foot.

1-4—Step diagonally forward with right foot and bounce two times.

5-8—Step diagonally forward with left foot and bounce two times.

On the last bounce, make a quarter turn to the left. Repeat the dance.

2. Eight Count

Description: An eight-count dance

Music: "Pink Cadillac," EMI Manhattan Records, B-50117.

Formation: Lines

Counts and Steps:

1—Right foot touch forward.

2—Right foot touch backward.

3—Right foot touch sideward.

4—Right foot touch forward.

5-7—Grapevine right, left, right with a half turn right.

8—Left foot close beside right foot.

Repeat the dance using the left foot to begin.

3. Ruby Baby

Description: An old-time line dance, created by New Jersey square dance caller, Mike Gilden

Music: Dion, "Ruby Baby," Columbia (or Capital), 13-33063.

Formation: All students facing front

Counts and Steps:

1-8—Right heel forward, right foot returns beside left foot; left heel forward, left foot returns beside right foot, and repeat.

1-4—Grapevine right, right foot, left foot, right foot, kick left foot forward with a quarter turn right.

5-8—Step backward four steps, left foot, right foot, left foot, right foot, touch the right foot on the last right.

Repeat the dance.

4. Alley Cat

Description: An American novelty dance, of uncertain origin

Music: "Alley Cat," ATCO Records, 45-6226.

Formation: Individual dancing with all students facing front

Counts and Steps:

1-2—Extend right foot to right side, touch toe to floor, and close right foot to left foot.

3-4—Extend right foot to right side, touch toe to floor, and close right foot to left foot, shift weight to right foot.

5-8—Repeat counts 1 to 4 with the left foot.

1-4—Repeat first set of counts 1 to 4 with right foot extended back.

5-8—Repeat second set of counts 1 to 4 with left foot.

1—Lift right foot straight up; let foot hang naturally about 8 inches from floor as if marching in place.

2—Touch right foot to floor, in place.

3—Repeat count 1.

4—Close right foot to left foot, shift weight to right foot.

5-8—Repeat third set of counts 1 to 4 with left foot.

1-2—Repeat third set of counts 3 and 4 with right foot.

3-4—Repeat fourth set of counts 1 and 2 with left foot.

5-6—Clap hands one time and hold.

7-8—Jump on both feet to make a quarter turn right.

Dance begins again. Dance is done eight times through, in the same way. Ninth time every movement is halved as follows:

1-2—Extend right foot to right side (1) and close (2).

3-4—Extend left foot to left side and close.

5-6—Extend right foot back and close.

7-8—Extend left foot back and close.

1-2—Lift right foot and close.

3-4—Lift left foot and close.

5-6—Clap both hands.

7-8—Quarter turn or bow.

5. Hustle

Description: This is a classic.

Music: "Axel F," MCA Records, MCA-52536.

Formation: Lines

Counts and Steps:

1-4—Walk backward steps; begin with right foot, transfer the weight to the left, the right, the left.

5-8—Walk forward steps; begin with left foot, right foot, left foot, right foot.

1-4—Grapevine to the right with right foot, left foot, right foot, and touch left foot to right foot.

5-8—Grapevine to the left with left foot, right foot, left foot, and touch right foot to left foot.

1-4—Hustle right; step right together with left foot, step right, touch with left foot beside right foot.

5-8—Hustle left; step left together with right foot, step left, touch with right foot beside left foot.

1-2—Snap fingers two times overhead.

3-4—Stomp right foot two times.

5-8—Right toe forward, backward, side, raise knee high, and make a quarter turn left.

Repeat the dance.

6. Jessie Polka

Description: An old-time dance done to country music

Music: "Jessie Polka," Folkcraft records, 1071-B.

Formation: Lines, dancers side-by-side, moving counterclockwise around the room

Counts and Steps:

1—Left heel forward.

2—Step left foot beside right foot.

3—Right toe back.

4—Touch right foot beside left foot.

5—Right heel forward.

6—Step right foot beside left foot.

7—Left heel forward.

8—Cross left foot in front of right foot.

1-8—Start on left foot; do four two-steps forward.

Repeat the dance.

7. Twelve Count

Description: This dance has only 12 steps.

Music: "The Heat Is On," MCA Records.

Formation: Lines

Counts and Steps:

1-2—Step right foot and close.

3-4—Step left foot and close.

5—Step forward on right foot.

6—Step forward with left foot behind right foot.

7—Step forward with right foot with a quarter turn right.

8—Kick left foot forward.

1—Step back on left foot.

2—Step back on right foot.

3—Step back on left foot.

4—Touch with right foot.

Repeat the dance.

8. Old Flame

Description: A country line dance with quarter turns

Music: "Old Flame," RCA, PB-12169.

Formation: Lines

Counts and Steps:

1-4—Step right foot to side and close left foot; shift weight to left foot. Step right foot to side and close left foot to right foot.

5-8—Step left foot to side and close right foot; shift weight to right foot. Step left foot to side and close right foot to left foot.

1-8—Right heel forward and close, left heel forward and close; right heel forward and close, and left heel forward and close.

1-8—Grapevine with the right foot to the right, four steps; and Grapevine with the left foot to the left, four steps.

1-8—Two two-steps forward and make a quarter turn right on third two-step.

Repeat the dance in lines, turning together.

9. Margie Dance

Description: This line dance was choreographed in honor of Margie Hanson and presented at a retirement tribute for her at the 1992 American Alliance for Health, Physical Education, Recreation and Dance (AAHPERD) National Convention.

Music: "I'd Like to Teach the World to Sing," Metromedia Records, KMD1051.

Formation: Lines

Counts and Steps:

1-2—Introduction, sway with body or hands.

3-4—Hands in air and sway to the right, left, right, and left.

5-8—Walk to right and give a high five greeting on step 8.

1-4—Walk to left and give a high five greeting on step 4.

5-8—Hands in air and sway to the right, left, right, and left.

1-4—Join and raise hands.

5-8—Lower hands.

1-4—"Thank you" in sign language (see Figure 4.1), two times.

5-8—"I love you" in sign language (hold two middle fingers down and keep pinky, index finger, and thumb up) and raise hands.

Repeat dance three more times. At the end, hug your neighbors in this world and give them some N and G's, which means tell them some nice and good things.

Figure 4.1   "Thank you" in sign language.

10. Popcorn

Description: A good dance to do to different kinds of music

Music: "Popcorn," Wind Dance, ERIC4009.

Formation: Lines

Counts and Steps:

1-8—Grapevine right and left.

1-2—Step forward on right foot and hop.

3-4—Step forward on left foot and hop.

5-8—Step backward on right foot, left foot, right foot, and kick with left foot.

1-2—Rock forward on left foot, two bounces.

3-4—Rock backward on right foot, two bounces.

5-8—Walk three steps forward on the left foot, right foot, left foot and a quarter turn on the left foot to the left.

Repeat the dance.

11. Hallelujah

Description: This can be a sing-along dance.

Music: "Hallelujah," Hit Parade, WBS 8877.

Formation: Lines

Counts and Steps:

1-4—Body sways as the hands raise and sway left, right, left, right.

5-8—Walk to the right; step left, right, left, right.

1-4—Body sways as the hands raise and sway left, right, left, right.

5-8—Walk to the left; step right, left, right, left.

1-4—Walk forward left foot, right foot, left foot; touch right heel forward and lean backward, with palms upraised in praise.

5-8—Walk backward right, left, right; touch left toe in back.

1-4—Walk forward left, right, cut left foot over right foot; step back on right foot.

5-8—Repeat fourth set of counts 1 to 4.

Repeat the dance.

LINE DANCE DESCRIPTIONS FOR THE INTERMEDIATE LEVEL

These line dances encourage development of movement patterns into repeatable sequences.

Intermediate Level Characteristics

Characteristics of learners at this level are expanded into three developmental areas: cognitive, affective, and psychomotor. Awareness of these characteristics assists us in planning lessons and units. They offer general guidelines, and in the classroom we will each make our final decisions based on specific needs.

Cognitive

- Develop patterns and movement combinations into repeatable sequences.
- Design dance sequences that are personally interesting.
- Recognize the cultural role of dance in understanding others.

Affective

- Appreciate differences and similarities in others' physical activity.
- Respect persons from different backgrounds and the cultural significance of the dances and rhythmic activities.
- Enjoy feelings from involvement in physical activity.

Psychomotor

- Maintain aerobic activity for a specified time.
- Create and perform dances that combine traveling, balancing, and weight transfer with smooth sequences and intentional changes in direction, speed, and flow.
- Participate vigorously for a sustained time while maintaining a target heart rate.

12. Soul Walk

Description: This is a dance of the early 1960s.

Music: "Let's Hear It for the Boy," Columbia, 38-04417.

Formation: Lines

Counts and Steps:

1-4—Step right foot to side, close left foot; step right foot to side and touch with left foot.

5-8—Step left foot to side, close right foot; step left foot to side and touch with right foot.

1-2—Touch right foot forward, touch right foot backward.

3-4—Step forward with right foot, make a quarter turn right.

5-6—Touch left foot to side, crossover right foot, and step with left foot.

7-8—Touch right foot to side, crossover left foot, and step with right foot.

Repeat the dance.

13. Double Side Step

Description: A high-energy modern dance

Music: "Rocket 2U," MCA Records.

Formation: Lines

Counts and Steps:

1-4—Step forward with right foot, touch left foot beside right foot, touch left foot to the side, return left foot beside right foot.

5-8—Step to the side with left foot, touch right foot beside left foot, touch right foot to the side, return right foot beside left foot.

1-4—Step to the side with right foot, touch left foot beside right, step to the side with the left foot, touch right foot beside left.

5-8—Grapevine to the right; make a half turn on count 7 to 8.

1-4—Step right foot forward, step left foot beside, step right foot forward, step left foot beside.

5-8—Step right foot backward, step left foot beside, step right foot forward, step left foot beside.

Repeat the dance.

14. New York, New York

Description: A show classic that adds a lot to a program

Music: "Theme from New York," MCA Records.

Formation: Individual and line

Counts and Steps:

1-8—Step left foot to side, kick right foot (see Figure 4.2), step right foot to side; kick left foot.

1-4—Four walking steps backward, left foot, right foot, left foot, kick right foot.

5-8—Four walking steps forward, right foot, left foot, right foot; kick left foot.

1-8—Step left foot to side, ball-change, left foot, then right foot; step right foot to side, ball-change, right foot, then left foot. Repeat two times.

1-4—Four steps turning to the left with left foot, right foot, left foot; touch right foot beside left foot.

5-8—Four steps turning to the right with right foot, left foot, right foot; touch left foot beside right foot.

Repeat the dance.

15. Louisiana Saturday Night

Description: This is a high-energy dance.

Music: "Don't Rock the Juke Box," Arista Records, AC-8681, 1991.

Formation: Lines

Counts and Steps:

1-8—Step right foot to the right, close left foot, step right foot to the right, close left foot, step right foot to the right, close left foot.

1-8—Step left foot to the left, close right foot, step left foot to the left, close right foot, step left foot to the left, close right foot.

1-8—Four step-kicks in place; step on right foot, kick left foot. Step on left foot, kick right foot. Step on right foot, kick left foot. Step on left foot, kick right foot.

1-4—Walk forward four steps, right foot, left foot, right foot; kick left foot two times.

5-8—Walk backward four steps, left foot, right foot, left foot; kick right foot two times.

Repeat the dance.

Figure 4.2 Step kicks start out *New York, New York.*

16. Little Black Book

Description: A classic old-time dance that can be done individually or with a partner

Music: "Little Black Book," Columbia Hall of Fame, 13-33051.

Formation: Line or partner dance

Counts and Steps:

1-8—Grapevine to the right on the right foot and Grapevine to the left on the left foot.

1-4—Two step-hops forward on the right foot and left foot.

5-8—Run forward, right foot, left foot, right foot, kick left foot, and pivot a quarter turn to the right.

1-4—Step backward three steps on left foot, right foot, left foot. On the fourth step, begin the dance on the right foot.

Repeat the dance.

17. Continental

Description: This is an old-time line dance of the 1950s.

Music: "Good Luck Charm," RCA 447-0636.

Formation: Lines

Counts and Steps:

1-8—Grapevine with the right foot to the right four steps and Grapevine with the left foot to the left four steps.

1-6—One two-step forward right foot, left foot, right foot, and one two-step forward left foot, right foot, left foot. Make a quarter turn to the right; kick out the right heel.

1-4—Five kicks; alternate right foot and left foot. On the fifth kick cross the right foot in front of the left foot. When the toe touches the floor, that is the 18th count.

Repeat the dance.

18. Bus Stop 1

Description: This is a classic that is always fun to do.

Music: "Old Time Rock and Roll," Capitol Records, B-5276.

Formation: Lines

Counts and Steps:

1-4—Begin with feet together; click heels together two times.

5-6—Right heel forward and touch two times.

7-8—Right toe backward and touch two times.

1-4—Right heel forward, right toe backward, right toe to the side. Raise knee high while making a quarter turn on the left foot; place the right foot beside the left foot.

5-8—Walk backward right foot, left foot, right foot, left foot.

1-4—Full turn to the right; step right foot, left foot, right foot, and touch left foot beside right foot.

5-8—Full turn to the left; step left foot, right foot, left foot, and touch right foot beside left foot.

1-4—Hustle right; step right foot together with left foot, step right foot, touch left foot beside right.

5-8—Hustle left; step left foot together with right foot, step left foot, touch right foot beside left.

Repeat the dance.

19. Electric Slide 1 The Boss

Description: This is a popular line dance from the 1980s.

Music: "Electric Boogie," Island Records, ZCM 126.

Formation: Lines

Counts and Steps:

1-4—Three slides to the right and close with left foot beside right foot.

5-8—Three slides to the left and close with right foot beside left foot.

1-4—Walk backward three steps; right foot, left foot, right foot and touch left foot beside right foot.

5-6—Step forward with the left foot, touch right foot beside left foot.

7-8—Step backward with the right foot, touch left foot beside right foot.

1-2—Step forward with the left foot; make a quarter turn to the left on the left foot. Touch right foot beside left foot.

Repeat the dance.

20. The Freeze

Description: A fun-filled dance to do with country music

Music: "San Antonio Stroll," MCA Records.

Formation: Lines

Counts and Steps:

1-4—Grapevine to the right and lift left foot on the fourth count.

5-8—Grapevine to the left and lift right foot on the eighth count.

1-4—Walk backward; right foot, left foot, right foot, lift left foot on the fourth count.

5-8—Rock forward on left foot for two counts and backward on the right foot for two counts.

1-2—Step forward on left foot; lift the right foot while making a quarter turn to the left on the left foot.

Repeat the dance.

21. Electric Slide 2 Hollywood Shuffle

Description: A second version of the Electric Slide provides variety for your class.

Music: "Electric Boogie," Island Records, ZCM 126.

Formation: Lines

Counts and Steps:

1-4—Touch right foot to side and close, two times.

5-8—Touch left foot to side and close, two times.

1-4—Touch right foot forward, backward, forward, with a quarter turn to right; touch left foot to side.

5—Touch left foot to side.

6—Cross left foot over right foot and step on left foot.

7—Touch right foot to side.

8—Cross right foot over left foot and step on right foot.

1-2—Step backward on left foot and close right foot beside left foot.

3-4—Jump in place and clap.

Repeat the dance.

22. Electric Slide 3

Description: A third version of the Electric Slide that is a great one to do

Music: "Electric Boogie," Island Records, ZCM 126.

Formation: Lines

Counts and Steps:

1-4—Touch right foot to side and close, two times.

5-8—Touch left foot to side and close, two times.

1-8—Touch right heel forward two times, touch right toe backward two times.

1-4—Touch right heel forward, toe backward, and step forward on right foot, make a quarter turn right.

5—Touch left foot to side.

6—Cross left foot over right foot; step on left foot.

7—Touch right foot to side.

8—Cross right foot over left foot; step on right foot.

1-2—Step backward left foot and close right foot beside left foot.

3-4—Jump a quarter turn to the right, two times.

5-8—Step backward on right foot, left foot, right foot, left foot.

Repeat the dance.

LINE DANCE DESCRIPTIONS FOR THE ADVANCED LEVEL

The advanced line dances use the body and movement to communicate ideas and feelings.

Advanced Level Characteristics

Characteristics of learners at this level are expanded into three developmental areas: cognitive, affective, and psychomotor. Awareness of these characteristics assists us in planning lessons and units. They offer general guidelines, and in the classroom we will each make our final decisions based on specific needs.

Cognitive

- Identify the proper warm-up, conditioning, and cool-down skills and their purposes.
- Describe techniques using body and movement activities to communicate ideas and feelings.
- Describe training and conditioning principles for specific dances and physical activities.

Affective

- Identify, respect, and participate with persons of various skill levels.
- Enjoy the aesthetic and creative aspects of performance.
- Respect physical and performance limitations of self and others.

- Enjoy meeting and cooperating with others during physical activity.

Psychomotor

- Perform simple folk, country, and creative dances.
- Sustain aerobic activity, maintaining a target heart rate to achieve cardiovascular benefits.
- Perform dances with fluency and rhythm.
- Participate in dance activities representing various cultural backgrounds.

23. Texas Bop

Description: A country line dance

Music: "Drivin' My Life Away," Elektra Records, E-45110-A.

Formation: Lines

Counts and Steps:

1-4—Left heel forward and close, two times.

5-8—Right toe rotates outward 90 degrees and in, two times.

1-4—Left heel forward and close, two times.

5-8—Right toe rotates outward 90 degrees and in, two times.

1-4—Both heels out and in, two times.

5-8—Right toe backward, right foot brush forward, right leg cross left knee, right foot brush forward.

1-2—Two-step right foot, left foot, right foot.

3-4—Two-step left foot, right foot, left foot.

5-6—Two-step right foot, left foot, right foot.

7-8—Stomp three times, right foot, left foot, right foot.

Repeat the dance.

24. Southside Shuffle

Description: This is a western dance done with facing lines.

Music: "I Love a Rainy Night," Elektra Records, E-45111-A.

Formation: Two lines facing; change sides at end on two-steps

Counts and Steps:

1-4—Right toe rotates outward 90 degrees (see Figure 4.3) and in with heel on floor, two times.

5-6—Right heel forward, touch two times.

7-8—Right toe backward, touch two times.

1-4—Right heel forward, right toe backward, right toe side, right foot kick up and behind left leg; slap right instep with left hand.

1-8—Grapevine to the right beginning on the right foot, Grapevine to the left beginning on the left foot.

Figure 4.3 Rotate your toe out to start the Southside Shuffle.

1-4—One two-step forward on right foot, left foot, right foot, with a half turn to the right on the right foot on count 24.

5-8—One two-step backward on left foot, right foot, left foot, and close right foot beside left with a stomp.

Repeat the dance.

25. Sports Dance

Description: This is a combination of sports moves.

Music: "When the Going Gets Tough."

Formation: Lines

Counts and Steps:

PART A:

1-16—Grapevine to the right beginning on the right foot, eight counts; Grapevine to the left beginning on the left foot, eight counts.

1-4—One two-step on right foot and rock-step backward on left foot; step forward on right foot.

5-8—One two-step on left foot and rock-step backward on right foot, step forward on left foot.

1-4—Repeat steps for second set of 1 to 4 counts.

5-8—Repeat steps for second set of 5 to 8.

PART B:

1-8—Schottische; step forward on right foot, left foot, right foot, hop on right foot.

1-4—Repeat steps for first set of counts 1 to 8 in Part A.

5-8—Schottische; step backward on left foot, right foot, left foot, hop on left foot.

1-8—Four quarter pivot turns to the right to complete the full turn.

1-8—Four quarter pivot turns to the left to complete the full turn.

Repeat the dance.

26. Rise

Description: A line dance of the 1970s

Music: "Rise," A&M Records.

Formation: Lines

Counts and Steps:

PART A:

1-4—Hustle right; step on right foot, together with left foot. Step right foot and touch with left foot.

5-8—Hustle left; step on left foot, together with right foot. Step left foot and touch with right foot.

1-4—Repeat steps for first set of counts 1 to 4.

5-8—Repeat steps for first set of counts 5 to 8.

1-4—Step forward on right foot, left foot, right foot, and hold one count.

5-8—Step forward on left foot, right foot, left foot and hold one count.

1-4—Step to the right side on the right foot and touch left, two times.

5-8—Step to the left side on the left foot and touch right, two times.

PART B:

1-4—Step backward on right foot, left foot, right foot; hold one count.

5-8—Step backward on left foot, right foot, left foot; hold one count.

1-8—Rock side to side; go down four counts and up four counts.

1-8—Step right foot forward; make a quarter pivot turn on right foot. Make four quarter turns back to the front.

1-8—Step left foot forward; make a quarter pivot turn on left foot. Make four quarter turns back to the front.

Repeat the dance.

27. Heel-and-Toe Rocky Bop

Description: A country dance

Music: "Touch a Hand, Make a Friend," MCA Records.

Formation: Lines

Counts and Steps:

1-2—Left heel forward and close.

3-4—Right toe backward and close.

5-6—Right heel forward, right foot cross left knee.

7-8—Right heel forward and close.

1-2—Left heel forward, left foot cross right knee.

3-4—Left heel forward and close.

1-8—Four forward two-steps; start on left foot.

Repeat the dance.

28. DPI Special

Description: This dance was created by John Bennett while at the North Carolina Department of Public Instruction.

Music: "Celebration," K-Tel, TU 2790.

Formation: Lines

Counts and Steps:

1-2—Right arm palm down, point two times to right.

3-4—Left arm palm down, point two times to left.

5-6—Right arm palm up, point two times to right.

7-8—Left arm palm up, point two times to left.

1-2—Right thumb, point two times over right shoulder.

3-4—Left thumb, point two times over left shoulder.

5-6—Roll hands in front while bending downward.

7-8—Roll hands in front while bending upward.

1-2—Right hand points to left knee, two times.

3-4—Left hand points to the right knee, two times.

5—Right hand slaps left knee, one time.

6—Left hand slaps right knee, one time.

7—Right hand slaps right hip, one time.

8—Left hand slaps left hip, one time.

1-3—Jump forward three times; cross feet on third.

4—Jump a quarter turn right; uncross legs.

Repeat the dance.

29. Bus Stop 2

Description: This is a variation on a classic.

Music: "Old Time Rock and Roll," Capitol Records, B-5276.

Formation: Lines

Counts and Steps:

1-4—Walk back four steps; start on right foot, left foot, right foot, left foot.

5-8—Walk forward four; start on left foot.

1-4—Repeat steps for first set of counts 1 to 4.

5-8—Repeat steps for first set of counts 5 to 8.

1-8—Grapevine, right and left.

1-2—Step right and touch left.

3-4—Step left and touch right.

5-8—Heels out and in, two times.

1-2—Touch right heel forward, two times.

3-4—Touch right toe backward, two times.

5-8—Touch right toe forward, backward, sideward, cross, and pivot a quarter turn to the left.

Repeat the dance.

30. The Rebel Strut

Description: A country dance with half turns

Music: "Sweet Country Music," MCA Records.

Formation: Lines facing front

Counts and Steps:

1-4—Right heel forward, cross right heel in front of left leg; right heel forward, right foot close.

5-8—Left heel forward, cross left heel in front of right leg; left heel forward, left foot close.

1-4—Right heel forward, right close; left toe backward, left close.

5-8—Step right forward and make a half turn; turn left to the rear. Step right forward and make a half turn; turn left to front.

1-8—Four forward two-steps; start on right.

Repeat the dance.

31. Slap 'n' Leather

Description: A great country classic

Music: "Crying My Heart Out Over You," Epic Records, 14-02692.

Formation: Lines

Counts and Steps:

1-4—Right toe point to side and together, two times.

5-8—Left toe point to side and together, two times.

1-2—Place right heel forward, two times.

3-4—Place right toe backward, two times.

5-6—Place right heel forward, side, back, side.

7—Touch right foot instep with left hand.

8—Touch right heel with right hand and make a quarter turn to the left.

1-8—Grapevine to the right, four steps and Grapevine left, four steps.

1-2—Step two steps backward, right, left, right, left.

3-4—Step forward on left foot, right foot; then stomp.

5-8—Two heel clicks; fan heels out and in two times.

Repeat the dance.

32. Tush Push

Description: This dance has much variety, and it is a four-wall dance.

Music: "Rainy Day Bells," Ripete, PV 15673.

Formation: Lines

Counts and Steps:

1-4—Right heel forward, right toe beside, and place right heel forward twice.

5-8—Left heel forward, left toe beside, and place left heel forward twice.

1-4—Bleking step; begin with right heel forward on count 1. Spring and place left heel forward on count 2. Spring and place right heel forward on count 3. Hold on count 4 and clap.

5-6—Rock forward and place weight onto right foot, bend knees and bounce at knee for two counts.

7-8—Rock back onto left foot and bounce at knee for two counts.

1-2—Rock forward onto right foot and bounce, then rock back onto left foot and bounce.

3-4—Repeat rock forward onto right foot and bounce, then rock back onto left foot and bounce.

5-6—Two-step forward; right foot, left foot, right foot.

7-8—Rock forward onto left foot, then rock back onto right foot.

1-2—Two-step backward; left foot, right foot, left foot.

3-4—Rock backward onto right foot, then rock forward onto left foot.

5-6—Two-step forward; right foot, left foot, right foot.

7-8—Step forward on left foot and make a half turn to right; transfer weight from left to right foot.

1-2—Two-step forward; left foot, right foot, left foot.

3-4—Step forward on right and make a half turn to left; transfer weight from right to left foot.

5-6—Make a quarter turn to face left wall by stepping on right and pivoting on left foot (transfer weight to left foot).

7-8—Stamp right foot beside left, then clap.

Repeat the dance.

SUMMARY

Three levels of line dances have been provided in this chapter to ensure that all students are included in this exciting dance form. Characteristics of each level have also been incorporated into the chapter to assist you in selecting your students' appropriate entry levels. Finally, each dance has been fully described to help you teach your students.

Line dances give students the opportunity to solo in a very nonthreatening manner. The flexibility of the dances in this chapter will allow students to be successful and give them the confidence to use them in a social setting.

CHAPTER 5

MIXERS

The mixer is one of the more exciting forms of rhythmic activities. Virtually all cultures around the world have their special mixers. They provide an opportunity to meet and greet people in an open, nonthreatening environment that focuses on the individual. This is a wonderful by-product of rhythmic and dance activities.

As people mature, it is critical that they find balance mentally, emotionally, physically, socially, and spiritually to ensure a lifetime of healthful living. Mixers provide many benefits in these areas, but perhaps their greatest contribution comes in the social realm. Their main purpose is to provide a nonthreatening environment for people to grow socially and safely. Give them a try; you may discover or rediscover that they have potential to enrich your program.

The following are all easy mixers for your classes. They will provide you with a wealth of information and enough depth to meet the needs of your program. They are arranged into three groups: beginner, intermediate, and advanced. They are all easy, so you can use them at any level.

LIST OF MIXERS IN THIS CHAPTER

MIXER DESCRIPTIONS FOR THE BEGINNER LEVEL

These dance mixers consist of simple techniques coordinated for the student's level of development. The dances are progressively structured, and if followed, students will learn basic skills and communication with others.

Beginner Level Characteristics

Characteristics of learners at this level are expanded into three developmental areas: cognitive, affective, and psychomotor. Awareness of these characteristics assists us in planning lessons and units. They offer general guidelines, and in the classroom we will each make our final decisions based on specific needs.

Cognitive

- Recognize that movement concepts are similar in a variety of skills.
- Identify appropriate behaviors in physical activities for participating with others.

Affective

- Enjoy participation alone and with others.
- Appreciate the benefits that accompany cooperation and sharing.
- Show consideration toward others in the physical activity setting.

Psychomotor

- Travel in different ways in a large group without bumping into others or falling.
- Distinguish among straight, curved, and zigzag pathways while traveling in various ways.
- Combine various traveling patterns in time to the music.
- Skip, hop, gallop, and slide using mature motor patterns.

1. Oh Suzanna

Description: An American mixer that allows the children to sing

Music: "Oh Suzanna," RCA, LPM 1623.

Formation: Single circle, facing center with a partner

Counts and Steps:

PART A:

1-4—Girls forward and backward.

5-8—Boys forward and backward.

1-8—Partners face for a Grand Right and Left, pull by to the seventh person.

PART B:

1-32—Promenade, seventh person for two full choruses.

Variation: Swing seventh person for one chorus, and promenade with the seventh person for the second chorus.

PART C:

1-32—Sing chorus, "Oh Suzanna, oh don't you cry for me, for I come from Alabama with my banjo on my knee," while promenading.

Repeat the dance.

2. Simple Double Circle

Description: An American dance that can be done as a mixer or a partnered dance

Music: "Stray Cat Strut," EMI America, B-8122.

Formation: Double circle facing LOD

Counts and Steps:

PART A:

1-8—Walk forward eight steps.

1-8—Walk backward eight steps.

PART B:

1-4—Walk forward four steps.

5-8—Walk backward four steps.

PART C:

1-2—Walk forward two steps.

3-4—Walk backward two steps.

PART D:

1-4—Step-kick two times; alternate right and left.

5-8—Step-kick two times; alternate right and left.

Variation:

1-8—Grapevine left four steps; begin on the left foot.

1-8—Grapevine right four steps; begin on the right foot.

1-16—Walk forward, eight steps backward, two steps.

1-16—Grapevine left and Grapevine right, two times.

1-16—Inside person, move up to next person and swing.

Repeat the dance.

3. Bouquet of Flowers and Scarf

Description: An old-time American mixer that uses a scarf and a bouquet of flowers

Music: "Moon River," Roper Records, JH-405-B.

Formation: Partners form a circle, boys on the inside facing out. Couples dance. Two individuals, a girl holding a bouquet of flowers and a boy holding a scarf, wander inside the circle of dancers (see Figure 5.1). The girl gives her bouquet to another girl, and the boy gives his scarf to another boy. Then they dance with the new person's partner. The new carriers repeat this procedure, both selecting someone else. The bouquet of flowers identifies the girl, and the scarf identifies the boy. Since the suggested music, "Moon River," is a waltz, everyone waltzes to the music. However, a polka, a two-step, or anything else that you prefer could be applied to this dance. This mixer may also be combined with other mixers to add excitement and make the activity a success.

Figure 5.1 Starting formation for the Bouquet of Flowers and Scarf mixer.

4. Broom Dance

Description: An American mixer that is fun over and over again

Music: "The Tennessee Waltz," Mercury, C-30025X45.

Formation: Couples dance while music plays. One person holds a broom as if dancing with it. When this person drops the broom on the floor, everyone switches to a new partner including the person holding the broom. Whoever is left over is now the new broom holder.

5. Fun Mixers

Description: Some fun variations on mixers allowing dancers to call for themselves

Music: "Jopat Special," Jopat Records, JP-501.

Formation: Double circle facing CCW, any number of dancers stand in the middle of the circle. Take turns calling the dance, partners hold hands.

Counts and Steps:

1-4—Begin with feet together. The caller may call for the inside or outside circle to move up or back two, three, four, or whatever number of steps selected.

1-16—Dancers go to the other side of circle and swing whomever they choose when the caller calls for the "cheaters swing."

1-16—People in center, move to outer circles and replace a partner. This person goes to center.

1-16—Promenade.

6. Clap and Stomp Three Times

Description: An American mixer that can always motivate a group

Music: "Boogie Grass Band," Rhythm Records, RR-121-B.

Formation: Double circle facing LOD

Counts and Steps:

1-2—Clap hands, three times.

3-4—Stomp foot, three times.

5-6—Repeat steps for counts 1 to 2.

7-8—Repeat steps for counts 3 to 4.

1-8—Walk eight steps forward.

1-8—Slide six times CCW, and walk to new partner.

1-8—Slide eight times in opposite direction.

Repeat the dance.

7. Paul Jones

Description: An American polka with many opportunities to be active

Music: "Beer Barrel Polka," RCA, 447-0148.

Formation: Double circle, girls on inside holding hands and facing out, boys on outside holding hands and facing in

Counts and Steps:

PART A:

1-16—All circle left.

PART B:

1-32—Boys freestyle girls around the room when the caller says, "Paul Jones."

PART C:

1-16—Back to the center and circle left.

Repeat the dance.

8. Riga Jig

Description: An English circle mixer for unlimited numbers

Music: "Mountain Dew," Chaparral Records, C-108-B.

Formation: Double circle facing LOD

Counts and Steps:

PART A:

1-16—Promenade for 16 steps and face partner.

1-4—Clap hands, three times and hold.

5-8—Slap knees, three times and hold.

1-8—Do-Si-Do, if you please.

PART B:

1-4—Move to the right.

5-8—Shake right hands with new partner.

1-4—Say "hello, hello, hello," or "hello, my name is _____."

Repeat the dance.

9. Angus Reel

Description: An American mixer that is great for large groups

Music: "Walking to Kansas City," Kalox, K-1028-B.

Formation: Partners form a double circle facing LOD.

Counts and Steps:

1-8—Promenade eight steps and face partner.

1-4—Back away from partner, four steps.

5-6—Three stomps.

7-8—Three claps.

1-8—Do-Si-Do partner.

1-8—Do-Si-Do corner.

Repeat dance with corner as new partner.

10. Big Set Mixer

Description: An American mixer in a Big Circle

Music: "Let the Good Times Roll," Rhythm Records, RR-162.

Formation: Partners form a circle, boys on the inside facing out.

Counts and Steps:

PART A:

1-8—Right-hand turn for eight counts.

1-8—Left-hand turn for eight counts.

1-8—Two-hand turn for eight counts.

1-8—Back-to-back Do-Si-Do for eight counts.

PART B:

1-16—Swing next girl on left for 16 counts.

1-16—Promenade for 16 counts.

Repeat the dance.

MIXER DESCRIPTIONS FOR THE INTERMEDIATE LEVEL

Dances have been selected for this level that will help participants advance with as much edge as possible. Intermediate dance patterns change with more regularity, and students must begin adapting their movements to other dancers much more quickly than in the beginner level.

Intermediate Level Characteristics

Characteristics of learners at this level are expanded into three developmental areas: cognitive, affective, and psychomotor. Awareness of these characteristics assists us in planning lessons and units. They offer general guidelines, and in the classroom we will each make our final decisions based on specific needs.

Cognitive

- Develop patterns and movement combinations into repeatable sequences.
- Design dance sequences that are personally interesting.
- Recognize the cultural role of dance in understanding others.

Affective

- Appreciate differences and similarities in others' physical activity.
- Respect persons from different backgrounds and the cultural significance of the dances and rhythmic activities.
- Enjoy feelings from involvement in physical activity.

Psychomotor

- Maintain aerobic activity for a specified time.
- Create and perform dances that combine traveling, balancing, and weight transfer with smooth sequences and intentional changes in direction, speed, and flow.
- Participate vigorously for a sustained time while maintaining a target heart rate.

11. Pop Goes the Weasel

Description: An American beginner level mixer

Music: "Pop Goes the Weasel," RCA, EPA-4138.

Formation: Variation 1: Double circle, with two couples facing each other

Counts and Steps:

1-8—Forward and backward singing, "Round and round the cobbler's bench, the monkey chased the weasel."

1-8—Two couples join hands and walk once around to left singing, "In and out and round about singing Pop Goes the Weasel."

1-8—Walk to the right eight steps.

1-8—Couple one pops under arch formed by couple two and faces a new couple.

Repeat the dance.

Formation: Variation 2: Sets of three join hands and face CCW

Counts and Steps:

1-8—All walk forward singing, "Round and round the cobbler's bench, the monkey chased the weasel."

1-8—Form a circle of three and walk left singing, "In and out and round about singing Pop Goes the Weasel."

1-8—Circle right eight more steps.

1-8—On the words "Pop Goes the Weasel," the center dancer is popped under an arch formed by the other two dancers to join the next couple.

Repeat the dance.

12. Circassian Circle

Description: An English circle mixer

Music: "Up Jumped the Devil," Lloyd Shaw Recordings, 200-45.

Formation: Single circle facing center

Counts and Steps:

PART A:

1-16—Walk forward into the circle and walk back out of the circle, two times.

1-8—Girls walk to center and back out of the circle.

1-8—Boys walk to center and back out to left-hand girl.

PART B:

1-8—Swing new partner by interlocking right elbows.

1-8—Swing new partner by interlocking left elbows.

1-16—Promenade new partner around the ring.

13. Lucky Seven

Description: A fun circle mixer

Music: "Heart of My Heart," Blue Star, 2143-B.

Formation: Single circle facing center

Counts and Steps:

PART A:

1-8—Circle left.

1-16—All to the middle and back, two times.

PART B:

1-16—Grand Right and Left.

1-8—Swing the seventh girl.

PART C:

1-16—Promenade.

Repeat the dance.

14. Nine Pin

Description: A square dance mixer done with an extra girl in the center of the square

Music: "Good Luck Charm," Rhythm Records, RR-161-B.

Formation: Square of four couples with an extra girl in center

Counts and Steps:

PART A:

1-32—Each boy swings girl in center of the square, the Nine Pin.

PART B:

1-4—Boys to center of the square with backs to center, and hold hands.

5-8—All five girls to outside of the square facing in, and hold hands.

1-16—All circle left.

1-8—When word "swing" is heard, girls take a boy and go back home. The left-over girl in the center is the new Nine Pin.

Repeat the dance.

15. Double Circle Roll Back

Description: This American mixer has a fun progression.

Music: "San Antone," Pro Records, 102050-B.

Formation: Double circle faces LOD, varsouvienne position. Partners stand side-by-side; girl is on boy's right, slightly in front of him. Boy's right arm is extended across in back of girl's right shoulder, and boy holds girl's raised right hand in his right hand. Girl's left arm is extended in front of boy's chest and girl holds boy's left hand in her left hand at shoulder height.

Counts and Steps:

PART A:

1-8—Begin with feet together, step right, kick left, step left, kick right, step right, kick left, step left, kick right.

1-8—Grapevine right and Grapevine left.

1-8—Repeat steps in first set of counts 1 to 8.

1-8—Repeat steps in second set of counts 1 to 8.

PART B:

1-8—Repeat steps in first set of counts 1 to 8, Part A.

1-8—Repeat steps in the second set of counts 1 to 8, Part A.

1-8—Swing partner.

1-8—Boys roll back to meet next girl.

Repeat the dance.

16. Sicilian Circle

Description: an English circle mixer

Music: "English Folk Dancing with the Southerners," Southerner's Records, Side 2, #11.

Formation: Double circle, with two couples facing each other

Counts and Steps:

PART A:

1-16—Four hands, twice around.

1-8—Right hand around.

1-8—Left hand around.

PART B:

1-8—Girls chain over.

1-8—Girls chain back.

1-8—Forward and back.

1-8—Forward again and pass on through to the next couple.

Repeat the dance.

17. Bingo

Description: A waltz tempo American circle mixer

Music: "Bingo Waltz," Aston Dance Records, RD-101-A.

Formation: A circle mixer, partner dance where all hold hands facing center, girls on the right of the boys

Counts and Steps:

PART A:

1-3—Balance in by stepping to center, and close.

4-6—Balance out by stepping back out, and close.

1-6—Roll the girl across by allowing her to turn left to face partner; then proceed to new position on old partner's left.

1-36—Repeat three more times.

PART B:

1-24—Boys face girl on their right, and girls face left doing two slides to the center and two slides back out, two times.

PART C:

1-24—Grand Right and Left on B, I, N, G, O. Still facing partners, take right hands and begin a Grand Right and Left. Everyone shouts "B" while taking right hands, "I" on taking left hands, "N" with right hands, and "G" with left hands. When meeting the fifth girl, swing and shout "OOOH!"

Repeat dance after the "O" in BINGO.

18. Patty-Cake Polka

Description: A high-energy American circle mixer that requires clapping coordination

Music: "Patty-Cake Polka," Lloyd Shaw Recordings, 227-45.

Formation: Double circle, partners facing

Counts and Steps:

1-4—Left heel and toe, left heel and toe.

5-8—Three slides left, counterclockwise.

1-4—Right heel and toe, right heel and toe.

5-8—Three slides right, clockwise.

1-16—Patty-Cake, right hands three times, left hands three times, both hands three times, on your knees three times.

1-4—Right elbow turn.

5-8—On to the next person on your left.

Repeat the dance.

19. Troika

Description: A Russian mixer dance in which the triple formation is done to imitate a sleigh drawn by three spirited horses

Music: "Troika," Rhythms Productions, CC 601-2.

Formation: The triple formation with three students standing in a straight line

Counts and Steps:

PART A:

1-4—Four running leaps forward, diagonally right.

5-8—Repeat to left.

1-8—Eight running leaps forward.

1-8—Keep hands joined. Left dancer runs in place as right dancer runs through arch formed by left dancer and center dancer, who follows under own left arm.

1-8—Repeat as right dancer runs in place while left dancer does the figure.

PART B:

1-32—Three dancers join hands in a circle. Run 12 steps clockwise and stamp three times; repeat counterclockwise. Instead of stamping, face direction of large circle. Dancers one and three form an arch while dancer two runs through to next couple (see Figure 5.2).

Repeat the dance.

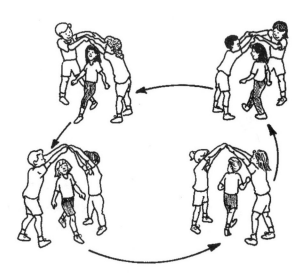

Figure 5.2 The center dancer moves up in the Troika Mixer.

20. Five-Foot Two

Description: An American mixer with fun music

Music: "Five-Foot Two," Lloyd Shaw Recordings, 45-122.

Formation: Double circle, facing LOD, varsouvienne position

Counts and Steps:

1-8—Two-step left, two-step right, walk four steps forward.

1-6—Two-step left, two-step right, walk two steps.

7-8—Release left hands and form a circle; boys face out, girls face in.

1-4—Balance forward, balance back.

5-8—Turn with the right hand, half around.

1-4—Balance forward, balance back.

5-8—Let go right hands and take the girl behind you.

Repeat the dance.

MIXER DESCRIPTIONS FOR THE ADVANCED LEVEL

These dances are selected to provide more challenge to the students who are willing and able to improve their dance skills.

Advanced Level Characteristics

Characteristics of learners at this level are expanded into three developmental areas: cognitive, affective, and psychomotor. Awareness of these characteristics assists us in selecting chapter content for planning lessons and units. They offer general guidelines, and in the classroom we will each make our final decisions based on specific needs.

Cognitive

- Identify the proper warm-up, conditioning, and cool-down skills and their purposes.
- Describe techniques using body and movement activities to communicate ideas and feelings.
- Describe training and conditioning principles for specific dances and physical activities.

Affective

- Identify, respect, and participate with persons of various skill levels.
- Enjoy the aesthetic and creative aspects of performance.
- Respect physical and performance limitations of self and others.
- Enjoy meeting and cooperating with others during physical activity.

Psychomotor

- Perform simple folk, country, and creative dances.
- Sustain aerobic activity, maintaining a target heart rate to achieve cardiovascular benefits.
- Perform dances with fluency and rhythm.
- Participate in dance activities representing various cultural backgrounds.

21. The Swinging Circle

Description: A clapping mixer

Music: "Swingin'," Warner Brothers Records, GWB 0446.

Formation: Single circle facing center

Counts and Steps:

PART A:

1-12—Boys walk to the center of the circle, join hands and circle left.

1-4—Drop hands and walk four steps to a new partner.

1-8—Swing for eight steps.

1-4—Clap hands, four times.

PART B:

1-12—Girls walk to the center of the circle, join hands and circle left.

1-4—Drop hands and walk four steps to a new partner.

1-8—Swing for eight steps.

1-4—Clap hands, four times.

Repeat the dance.

22. Oregon Mixer

Description: An American double circle mixer

Music: "Stray Cat Strut," EMI America, B-8122.

Formation: Partners in double circle, facing LOD

Counts and Steps:

PART A:

1-16—Schottische forward and backward, two times.

1-16—Grapevine right and left, two times.

PART B:

1-4—Face partner, hand clap with partner, right hand, left hand, right hand, left hand.

5-8—Two hip-bumps; right hip, right hip, left hip, left hip.

1-2—One shoulder-bump; right shoulder, left shoulder.

3-4—One knee-bump; right knee, left knee.

1-8—Back apart four steps and together four steps.

1-8—Grapevine right and Grapevine left.

1-4—Each person move to next person on the right for a new partner.

Repeat the dance.

23. Elvira

Description: An American mixer to country music

Music: "Elvira," MCA Records, MCA-51084.

Formation: Double circle faces LOD; holding inside hands, use opposite footwork.

Counts and Steps:

1-8—Swing your partner.

1-4—Boys begin on the left foot; girls begin on the right foot, forward two two-steps.

5-8—Grapevine away from partner, kick and clap on count 8.

1-4—Grapevine toward partner, clap right hands on count 4.

5-8—Turn away in small circle; boys turn left, girls turn right. Boy turns to the girl behind him, girls turn in place.

1-7—Join two hands with new partner, swing for five counts. Step back on right foot for boys and left foot for girls; close left foot for boys and right foot for girls.

8—Step forward on right for boys and left for girls.

24. Sweet Georgia Brown

Description: An American mixer that people of all ages like because of the music

Music: "Sweet Georgia Brown or the Aston Polka," Lloyd Shaw Recordings.

Formation: Double circle facing LOD

Counts and Steps:

1-4—Walk four steps.

5-8—Apart four steps.

1-4—Together four steps.

5-8—Right elbow turn for four steps.

1-4—Walk four steps.

5-8—Right elbow turn for four steps.

1-4—Left elbow turn for four steps.

5-8—Boy moves ahead to next girl in four steps.

Repeat the dance.

25. White Silver Sands

Description: An American round dance mixer

Music: "White Silver Sands," Grenn, 15006.

Formation: Couples holding inside hands, face LOD.

Counts and Steps:

PART A:

1-8—Walk forward three steps and turn half around, walk backward four steps.

1-8—Walk forward three steps and turn half around, walk backward four steps.

1-4—Balance away, balance together.

PART B:

1-8—Walk forward three steps and turn half around, walk backward four steps.

1-8—Walk forward three steps and turn half around, walk backward four steps.

PART C:

1-4—Balance away, balance together.

5-8—Circle away, boy to girl behind to butterfly position. Boy's left hand to girl's right hand and boy's right hand to girl's left hand with arms held out to the side.

1-4—Balance left, balance right.

Repeat the dance.

26. Oklahoma Mixer

Description: An American mixer

Music: "Old Southern Schottische," Shaw, 153. "Josephine," Shaw, 227.

Formation: Circle of couples in varsouvienne position, sweetheart position, face LOD. Both start with left foot.

Counts and Steps:

1-4—Two-step with left foot (see Figure 5.3), two-step with right foot.

5-8—Four walking steps forward, starting with left foot.

1-4—Partners facing, both do a left heel-and-toe diagonally forward, toward the left. Release right hands, girls walk left foot, right foot, left foot toward center of room, and boys walk left foot, right foot, left foot toward wall.

Figure 5.3   Starting formation for the Oklahoma Mixer.

5-8—Both do a right heel-and-toe. Release left hands, girls take three steps; right foot, left foot, right foot diagonally to outside of circle. Make a left-face turn to face LOD. Boys walk three steps forward to assume varsouvienne position with a new girl.

Repeat the dance.

27. Teton Mountain Stomp

Description: An American mixer

Music: "Teton Mountain Stomp," Windsor, 4615-A.

Formation: Single circle, partners facing and holding hands

Counts and Steps:

1-4—Begin on inside foot, step, close, step and stomp.

5-8—Repeat to outside.

1-2—Move in, step and stomp.

3-4—Move out, step and stomp.

5-8—Walk forward four steps with your partner, right hip to right hip.

1-4—Each person does a half turn with the boys going backward four steps and the girls forward four steps.

5-8—Reverse and walk four.

1-4—Turn and back up four.

5-8—Forward four to a new partner.

Repeat the dance.

28. CJ Mixer

Description: This exciting American mixer coordinates a lot of group action.

Music: "CJ Mixer," Lloyd Shaw Recordings, 3310.

Formation: Double circle facing LOD, varsouvienne position

Counts and Steps:

1-8—Walk forward three steps, turn halfway around, walk backward three steps.

1-8—Walk forward three steps, turn halfway around, walk backward three steps.

1-6—Left-Hand Star for six steps with girl in the lead.

7-8—Release hands and turn on steps 7 and 8, to RLOD.

1-6—Right-Hand Star for six steps.

7-8—Boys take the next girl on steps 7 and 8, turn to LOD.

Repeat the dance.

29. Tennessee Wig-Walk

Description: An American Southwest mixer that originated in the 1940s

Music: "The Tennessee Wig-Walk," MCA Recordings, MCA-60051.

Formation: Single circle, partners facing, boys face CCW and girls face CW. Everyone join right hands with a partner.

Counts and Steps:

PART A:

1-8—Touch left foot forward and side, Grapevine right and hold; partners change to left hands.

1-8—Touch right foot forward and side, Grapevine left and hold.

PART B:

1-8—Hold right hands; go around in a clockwise circle with a Schottische step or a L, R, L-hop, and a Schottische step or R, L, R-hop.

1-8—Boys progress forward, counterclockwise with a step-hop on left and a step-hop on right. The second girl he comes to as a new partner. Girl does the same moving clockwise to meet second boy as a new partner.

Repeat the dance.

30. La Bastringue

Description: A French-Canadian mixer

Music: "La Bastringue," Worldtone Records, WT 10034.

Formation: Single circle facing center with the girls on the boys' left sides

Counts and Steps:

PART A:

1-16—Forward and back, two times.

1-8—Circle left, using four two-steps.

1-8—Circle right, using four two-steps.

PART B:

1-4—Boys turn their left-hand girl; boy turns girl once CW under joined boy's left and girl's right hands with four walking steps to end facing in a closed position.

5-16—Partners swing.

1-16—Promenade eight two-steps. End in a single circle putting the girls on the boys' right sides.

Repeat the dance.

SUMMARY

Mixers focus on the important element of social fitness. The mixers in this chapter have been arranged for your students to be comfortable with the progressions in the dances. They will meet many other students without staying with any person a long time. These dances are simple, so students will have a high level of success and will come back wanting more.

CHAPTER 6

SQUARE DANCE AND CLOGGING

American Square Dance is an integral part of our heritage in the U.S.A. It is a popular dance form and has one of the highest participatory rates of all physical activities.

Its followers are many and for this reason, we begin with a short, informative historical section. The history of the American Square Dance helps us to revitalize, to reflect on our roots, and to see that we have historically been a nation of great dancers. Most important, we can bring our curriculum and heritage to life through dance. We then move into a section on teaching square dance to others. Here we deal with teaching suggestions, square dance calling, the square dance lesson, styling tips for the teacher and dancers, reminders for callers, and reminders for effective teaching.

The following sections deal with three types of square dancing. The first form is Appalachian Big Set, also known as Big Set. This is square dancing in sets of four persons and preceded the development of western square dance. The second form is western square dance. This section includes 10 lessons that will fit with all levels of dancers. It has to be modified only to meet the speed at which the group learns. The third form is clogging. It follows the western square dance, because dancers may clog dance in both the Appalachian Big Set form and the western square dance forms depending on where they live. However, smooth dancing or simply walking through the figures is the predominant form of dancing Appalachian Big Set and western square dance.

The Suggested Resources section at the end of the book includes information about obtaining music and directions for the activities in this chapter.

HISTORY OF AMERICAN SQUARE DANCE

On June 1, 1982, by act of the United States Congress, contemporary western square dance became the official American folk dance. The evolution of contemporary western square dance provides a history that parallels the development of our country as we know it today.

Since most early settlers of the eastern seaboard wanted nothing to do with their "mother countries," they preserved the cultures and dances of their new country.

In contemporary western square dance we have the vestiges of these early forms. The French Quadrille was a circle of eight and was danced primarily with visiting couples. The Appalachian Big Set, square dancing for circles of four with a circle large enough for any number of people, preceded the square of eight that we know today.

The Appalachian Big Set, the French Quadrille, and the Kentucky Running Set combined to form western square dancing. The term "western" was added because the dance was performed farther west as our country was settled. The western square dance with a circle of eight evolved into our contemporary western square dance form. It is referred to as western square dance to differentiate it from other forms of square dancing that are alive today.

Since teaching the Appalachian Big Set helps students learn western square dance patterns, it has been included before the western square dance section. It is a vehicle for starting new groups and provides a successful system for teaching square dancing to K-2 students.

During the evolution of the Appalachian Big Set and western square dance, dancers began stomping and shuffling their feet using what was referred to as clogging. Clogging has roots in virtually all the countries that had settled along the eastern seaboard. It has been included after the western square dance section because of its prevalence in our country and its great physiological benefits. It is a fun alternative to the more common smooth dancing or walking patterns seen in contemporary western square dancing.

BASICS OF TEACHING SQUARE DANCE

The following ingredients are important in developing your square dance program. They appear below in four sections: (a) Teaching Suggestions, (b) Square Dance Calling, (c) Designing the Square Dance Lesson, and (d) Styling Tips for Teacher and Dancers. The fourth section concludes with two checklists. One is reminders for callers, and the other is reminders for effective teaching.

Teaching Suggestions

There are a number of points to consider when teaching square dance. The following list has been compiled to assist you in making decisions about how to deliver your program.

- Start with the simplest move, then add the next simplest and see what variations you can do. Add a third when appropriate, never teaching too many at one time.
- The caller should strive to be the best possible square dancer before teaching others.
- Moves should be taught, retaught, and reviewed in succeeding sessions to ensure that the dancers know the moves.
- Reinforce in a positive manner.
- Start with a big circle for teaching the early moves.
- To keep the dancer's attention, mix the squares regularly in the beginning.
- Learning time should be fun time, full of discovery and excitement at each session. Don't just say that square dancing is fun—*show it!*
- If possible, callers should avoid using cue cards so their eyes can be on the dancers.
- Use costumes, scenery, and square dance songs to stimulate interest and a deeper understanding of the history and people who began this type of folk dancing.
- Teach the dance by phrases rather than by counts because this is less confusing to the dancers.
- Avoid spending too much time on one dance.
- Emphasize fun and enjoyment rather than the perfection of every skill.
- The caller must call within the framework of the dancer's knowledge.
- Discourage the dancers from clapping and stomping as their skills improve, so everyone can hear the calls and concentrate on the movements.
- When the square gets lost, instruct the dancers to return to their home positions and wait for the next call to start.

Square Dance Calling

Square dancing is directed by a caller. With very little practice, you can become proficient enough in square dance calling to conduct classes for beginners.

There are two basic calls in square dance, the patter call and the singing call. In the patter call, the caller directs the dancers through many formations that eventually bring them back to their home positions. Patter calling presents an element of surprise to the dancers. They don't know what sequence the caller is following and this challenges their skills.

The second variation is the singing call. It usually has seven choruses, all of which are sung. They have an opening figure, a main figure with the head two couples for two verses, a break, a main figure with the side two couples for two verses, and an ending. The opening, break, and ending contain the same figure with no partner change. The main figures have four partner changes to get dancers back to their original partners in their original positions.

Designing the Square Dance Lesson

A lesson could be divided into three or four parts. Part one is a warm-up time, a review of the movements learned to this point, and perhaps a full dance with these basic movements. Parts two and three could be combined or separated. If done separately, part two is the introduction of new moves with a walk-through and practice calls. Part three is one or more dances containing these new moves. Part four is the closing of the lesson. It is a time for the class to do previously learned dances and to request their favorites.

Styling Tips for Teachers and Dancers

Here are a few points regarding quality in the dance. Quality is the most important word to remember during your square dance time. How much you know is not as important as how well you know it. Dancers should be taught consideration for others. An antiroughness attitude must be maintained at all times. Dancers should help each other rather than pulling someone along. Dancers need to discover that at first they must "learn to listen." They can then "listen to learn," which is the nature of all dancing.

The term "styling" refers to all the points mentioned so far. Styling gives your dancers and dances quality. It starts with posture. Dancers should be reminded to stand tall—the "sitting room" is tucked under, and the "dining room" is held in tight. This posture is maintained throughout the dance as the dancers use a movement called a "shuffle" to travel through the moves. The shuffle is an easy, light walk in time to the music with the weight kept on the balls of the feet. The feet will be lightly in contact with the floor throughout most of a dance, and dancers will be encouraged to take small steps. The shuffle is the predominant locomotor pattern for square dancing. Clogging, another locomotor pattern, will be included later in the chapter as well.

Before starting a dance, it is customary to honor your partners and honor your corners. It is often called, "bow to your partners and corners." Usually the boys bow and the girls curtsy, or both can do a simple bow.

Use simple mixers in the beginning of lessons to get everyone dancing and having fun. Several simple mixers have been included in the western square dance section, not only to add variety and fun to a class, but also to reinforce learned moves and to introduce new moves.

The Appalachian Big Set, also known as "Big Circle," method of teaching skills is an excellent point to start your square dance lessons. The western square dance lessons will follow, and the Clogging section will complete the chapter.

The following lists serve as reminders for delivering your square dance program. Follow these suggestions as you build your program.

Reminders for Callers

- Be a motivator.
- Be enthusiastic.
- Be a leader and a good host or hostess.
- Set achievable goals.
- Practice so you sound good from the start.
- Use variety in your calls.
- Change the inflection of words at the ends of phrases to avoid becoming monotonous.
- Make it sound nice.
- Use a cadence and rhythm that corresponds to the record.
- Practice until calling becomes easy.

As was mentioned earlier, there are two kinds of calls, the patter call and the singing call. When using a singing call, remember that songs usually have a 64-beat chorus or sometimes an 80-beat chorus. If it has 80 beats, have the girls chain over and back to fill the extra 16 beats.

Reminders for Effective Teaching

- Always be simple—teach only what dancers have to know for that particular time.
- Instruct with patience, understanding, and compassion.
- Use clear, concise, and correct explanations.
- Use a show-and-tell format.
- Use practice and repetition.
- Plan your work and work your plan.
- Remain flexible, and be ready to take advantage of the "teachable moment."
- Repeat basics from various positions.
- Give lots of encouragement to dancers.
- Teach slowly.

APPALACHIAN BIG SET

Appalachian Big Set, as it is commonly called today, goes by the names Big Set, Big Circle, Big Circle Mountain. It is even known by some folks as the Running Set or Kentucky Running Set. It is designed to include any number of couples in a big circle, versus a square of four couples as in western square dance. The Big Set is the ideal place to begin square dancing fundamentals with your K-2 students. It allows everyone to see one another, so each can learn from the other, and it provides successful experiences from the beginning.

Whatever name you know it by, there are many figures done in this style dancing. We are indebted to this form for giving us many of our western square dance figures of today. It goes well before your western square dance because both forms have many of the same figures. It is best suited for your K-2 students, but can also serve as an appropriate introduction to western square dance for the 3-5 and 6-8 grade levels in your program.

In the Big Set the action goes around the set rather than across it. Movements for squares of eight can be separated from Big Set figures according to whether they are performed across the set or around the set. However, there are numerous moves in western square dance that go around the set. The Big Set is one big round dance for all those who want to join in the fun.

The early Big Set had and still has a caller, which is America's only unique contribution to square dance. If the calling was from within the set, it was quite simple and was considered a prompt. However, if the caller was outside the set, there was plenty of improvised patter added to the call.

This form of dancing is simple enough for everyone to enjoy, yet in its simplicity, quite lovely to watch.

Big Set usually has three parts: opening Big Set figures, Small Circle figures consisting of four people, and closing Big Set figures. Everyone dances the Big Circle figures together. Only two couples dance the Small Circle figures together; this is also known as a four-person square.

Big Circle Figures

It is important to know which person does what in the square dances, so your students should know about Big Circle identification. The girl on the boy's immediate right is his partner, and the next girl to the right is his right-hand girl. The girl to his left is his corner or left-hand girl (see Figure 6.1). *Note:* It is not imperative to pair boys with girls. Pairs can be boy–boy or girl–girl, or you can

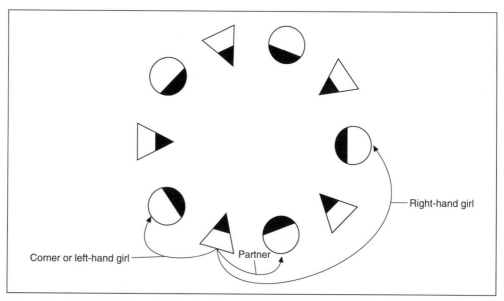

Figure 6.1   Big Circle identification.

use colored pinnies (or vests, or ribbons, or scarves) to differentiate partners; then do the calls by colors.

When dancing in small circles, couples can move into these circles of four in a variety of ways. One way is for couples to number off odd and even. One of the couples travels to the next couple to dance another figure. A second way is to couple up with four people. Those with their backs to the inside of the hall travel, and those on the outside stay in place. Third, the caller can have people couple up four hands (people) around and progress wherever they please as the caller directs.

Small Circle Figures

Big circle figures involve everyone in one large circle, whereas Small Circle figures are done with groups of four to eight people in them. When dancing the Small Circle figures and when two couples meet, they automatically join hands and circle left, even if the caller hasn't made the call. To get to circles of four, the caller may call, "odd couple out and circle up four," or "couple up four hands around."

Square Figures

A square consists of four couples facing center with the back of each dancer parallel to a different wall. Opposite couples are 7 to 10 feet apart from each other, and the girl is on the right of the boy.

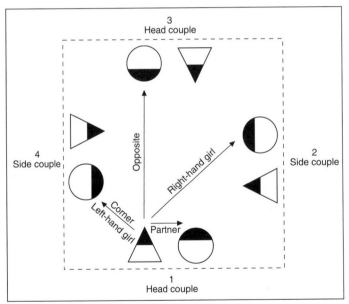

Figure 6.2 Square identification.

The couples are numbered one, two, three, four around the square in a CCW (counterclockwise) direction, starting with the couple whose back is to the front of the hall and the caller (see Figure 6.2). Couples one and three are the head couples, and couples two and four are the side couples. The girl on the boy's immediate right is his partner and the next girl to the right is his right-hand girl. The girl across the set is his opposite and the girl to his left is his corner or left-hand girl.

A successful method of teaching square dance moves is known as the "talk-through, walk-through, dance-through" approach. This means that you describe what you want your dancers to do using a demonstration if possible. Then everyone walks through the figure without music, and then, we dance through!

Note: The walk, honors, and square identification need to be included in the first session. The walk or shuffle and honors have already been described in the Big Set section.

LIST OF SQUARE DANCE FIGURES IN THIS CHAPTER

Advanced Level

SQUARE DANCE DESCRIPTIONS FOR THE BEGINNER LEVEL

This section includes both Big Circle and Small Circle figures. Your K-2 students may not master all of them, but by the end of the fourth year with this material, your students should be ready for the square figures.

Beginner Level Characteristics

Characteristics of learners at this level are expanded into three developmental areas: cognitive, affective, and psychomotor. Awareness of these characteristics assists us in planning lessons and units. They offer general guidelines, and in the classroom we will each make our final decisions based on specific needs.

Cognitive

- Recognize that movement concepts are similar in a variety of skills.
- Identify appropriate behaviors in physical activities for participating with others.

Affective

- Enjoy participation alone and with others.
- Appreciate the benefits that accompany cooperation and sharing.
- Show consideration toward others in the physical activity setting.

Psychomotor

- Travel in different ways in a large group without bumping into others or falling.
- Distinguish among straight, curved, and zigzag pathways while traveling in various ways.
- Combine various traveling patterns in time to the music.
- Skip, hop, gallop, and slide using mature motor patterns.

Big Circle Figures

1. Circle Left and Right

Designated dancers join hands to form a circle and move CW to the left (see Figure 6.3), or CCW to the right. If the caller does not specify which direction to circle, it is automatically circle left.

Styling: When hands are joined, boy's palms are up and the girl's palms are down. The elbows are bent comfortably so the hands are above the elbows.

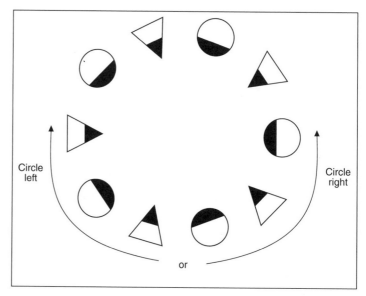

Figure 6.3   Circle left and right.

2. Forward and Back

The designated dancers move forward three steps, stop and touch (see Figure 6.4); then they back up three steps, stop and touch.

Styling: As couples come together holding inside hands, they may touch outside hands with the opposite couple on count 4, then back up.

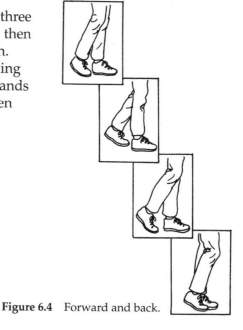

Figure 6.4   Forward and back.

3. Do-Si-Do

Two dancers face each other. As they walk around each other back to where they started, they pass right shoulders first, then back-to-back, then left shoulders (see Figure 6.5).

Count: Eight steps

Styling: Arms are in a natural position throughout the movement.

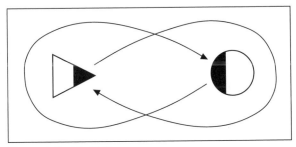

Figure 6.5   Do-Si-Do.

4. Swing

Two dancers standing right side to right side (hip-to-hip), move forward and around, turning CW (see Figure 6.6).

Figure 6.6   Keep your partner on your right side during your swing.

Count: Four steps for one turn or eight steps for two turns

Styling: Swing is done with right hips adjacent in a modified closed position. Boy's left hand holding girl's right, and the boy's right hand just above girl's waist on her back. The girl's left hand on the boy's right arm or shoulder. The buzz step swing is a pivoting action around the right feet of the dancers with the left foot acting as a pusher. The dancers lean back slightly and stay in close at the bottom. At the K-2 level, have students hold hands and walk around in a circle for their swing.

5. Couple Promenade

Two dancers walk in skater's position, side-by-side, left hands together and right hands together in front of the dancers. The girl on the right moves around the set CCW, unless otherwise indicated. Couples move back to their home positions and face the center of the set.

Styling: In the promenade position (see Figure 6.7), the boy's palms are up and the girl's are down. The boy's left forearm is over the girl's left arm. For K-2 children, holding hands works well for the promenade.

Figure 6.7   Promenade position.

6. Single-File Promenade

The dancers move one behind the other in a single circle (see Figure 6.8) either CCW right or CW left.

Styling: Hands and arms are in a natural position while walking around the set.

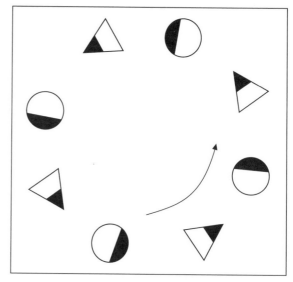

Figure 6.8   Single-File Promenade.

7. Single-File, Girl in the Lead

Same call as Single-File Promenade where the girl promenades in front of her partner around the circle CCW (see Figure 6.9).

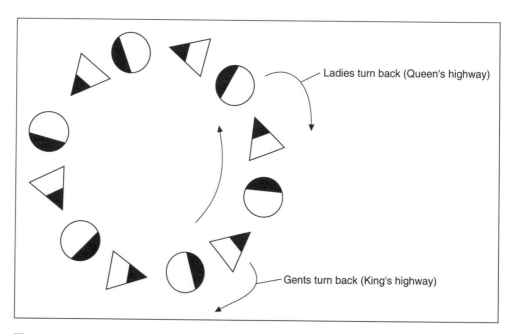

Figure 6.9   Single-File, Girl in the Lead.

8. Ladies Turn Back or Queen's Highway, Gents Turn Back or King's Highway

Both of these calls are executed from the Single-File, Girl in the Lead (see Figure 6.9). Either the girls or the boys, depending on the call, do a half turn to their right and promenade back around the outside of the circle CW until they meet their original partner or whomever the caller designates.

9. Girls to the Center, Boys to the Center, Everybody to the Center

Depending on whom the call is for, the designated dancers take four steps to the center of the circle and four steps back (see Figure 6.10).

10. Wind Up the Ball of Yarn

This call occurs when the caller indicates a designated dancer to "wind it up," as a snail's shell is wound, or like winding a ball of yarn from the outside in. The designated dancer releases his or her right hand to the next person, winds it up, turns in the opposite direction, and unwinds the figure (see Figure 6.11).

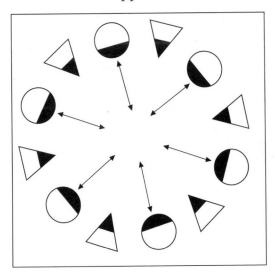

Figure 6.10   Girls to the Center.

Figure 6.11   Wind Up the Ball of Yarn.

11. Open Tunnel and London Bridge

For Open Tunnel the lead couple, while promenading, turns back. All the couples behind them form an arch for the leads to duck under (see Figure 6.12). Each succeeding couple then turns and ducks under the arch. When the lead couple gets through everyone, they form an arch and come back over the other dancers. Each succeeding couple does the same thing.

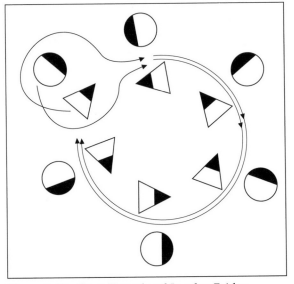

Figure 6.12   Open Tunnel and London Bridge.

If the call London Bridge is given, instead of going back under the arch, the lead couple turns and forms an arch with other couples following, just as the tunnel through call is done.

Small Circle Figures

12. Birdie in the Cage

One girl, usually the traveling girl, gets in the center of the other three dancers who circle around her (see Figure 6.13). Then the call "Bird fly out and crow hop in" may be given as the girl gets out of the circle. The traveling boy goes into the center while the other three circle with hands joined.

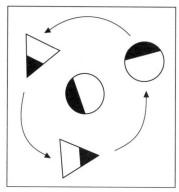

Figure 6.13   Birdie in the Cage.

13. Swing at the Wall

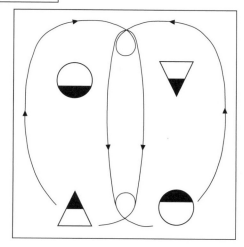

Inside couple around the outside and swing at the wall, then through that couple and swing in the hall (see Figure 6.14).

Figure 6.14   Swing at the Wall.

14. Take a Little Peek

Inside couple peek around sides of outside couple, back to the center and swing. Inside couple peek once more, back to the center and swing all four (see Figure 6.15).

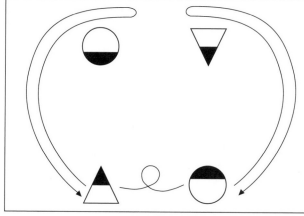

Figure 6.15   Take a Little Peek.

15. Mountaineer Loop

Inside couple drops inside hands and dives under and through an arch formed by the outside couple (see Figure 6.16). The inside couple comes back and joins hands. Then circle left and the figure is repeated by the outside couple under the inside couple's arch.

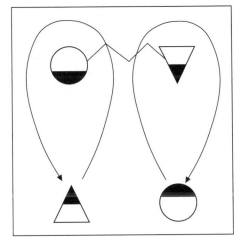

Figure 6.16   Mountaineer Loop.

16. Swing When You Meet

Inside couple around the outside couple and swing when you meet; back to the center and inside couple swings (see Figure 6.17). Inside couple around this couple once more and swing when you meet, back to the center and swing all four.

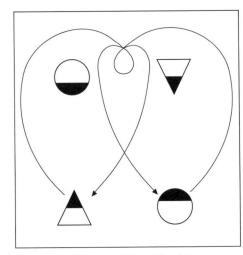

Figure 6.17   Swing When You Meet.

17. Couple Couples Swing

Inside couple through outside couple and go back home around the outside (see Figure 6.18). Couples swing their partners, then couple up four, circle four hands around.

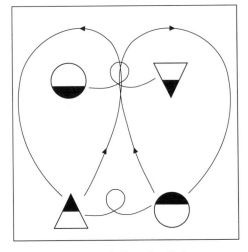

Figure 6.18   Couple Couples Swing.

18. Girl Around the Girl

Inside girl walks around the outside girl and the inside boy follows (see Figure 6.19a). Then inside girl walks around the outside boy and the inside boy doesn't go (see Figure 6.19b).

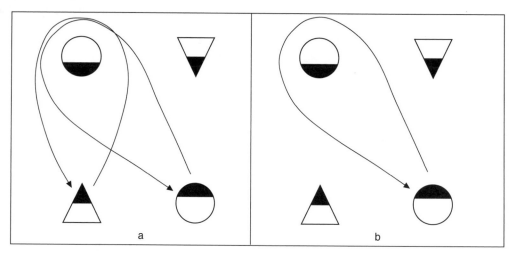

a   b

Figure 6.19   Girl Around the Girl.

19. Georgia Rang Tang

Turn your opposite partner with a right-hand around; turn your partner with a left-hand around (see Figure 6.20). Turn your opposite partner with a right and your partner with a left.

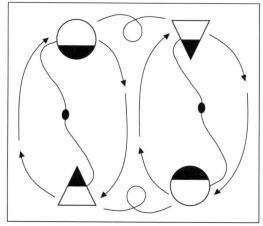

Figure 6.20   Georgia Rang Tang.

20. Allemande Left and Right

Two dancers holding either left or right hands walk around each other and back to place (see Figure 6.21). The Allemande Left is done with one's corner.

Count: Eight steps

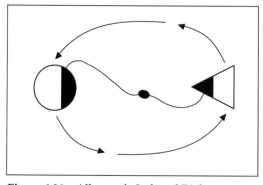

Figure 6.21   Allemande Left and Right.

21. Arm Turns, Left and Right

Two dancers holding either left or right forearms, walk around each other and back to place.

Count: Eight steps

Styling: Dancers grasp each other just below the elbow for this turn and walk around each other (see Figure 6.22).

Figure 6.22   Right-hand arm turn.

22. Grand Right and Left

Partners face and join right hands; pull that person by and give a left hand to the next. Boys go CCW and the girls go CW. Then another right and a left until each dancer meets original partner (see Figure 6.23).

23. Star Right and Left

Designated dancers step forward, extend either the right or left hand to form a star, and walk forward in the direction they are facing. Stars may be directed to turn a quarter, a half, three quarters, or a full turn.

Styling: Stars may be formed with palms up and touching in the center (see Figure 6.24) or as a wrist-hold star, in which each dancer holds the wrist of the person in front, a little lower than shoulder height.

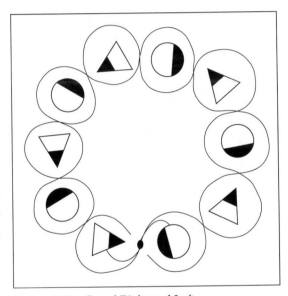

Figure 6.23   Grand Right and Left.

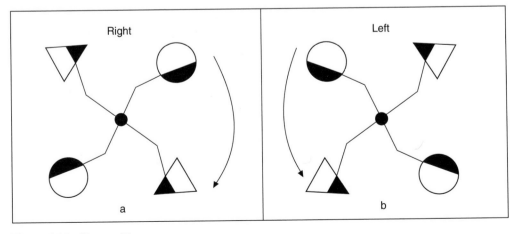

Figure 6.24   Star position.

24. Star Promenade

Same formation as a four-hand Star, except that those in the star place their arms around the designated dancer's waist and take that dancer with them (see Figure 6.25).

Styling: Both dancers put their arms around each other's waists in this movement.

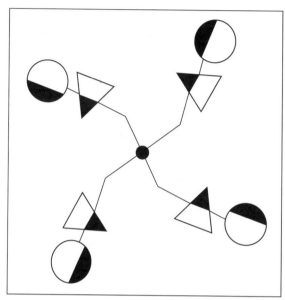

Figure 6.25   Star Promenade.

Practice Calls for the Beginner Level

All moves except the honors should be given 8 to 16 counts. Both the honors can be completed in eight counts. In the beginning, do not rush your students through the figures. Eventually, as their levels of expertise and confidence get higher, you will be able to get your students completing the moves in eight counts.

Sample Practice Call

Honor your partners.
Honor your corners.
All join hands and circle left.
Now circle to the right.
You all go forward and back.
Then Do-Si-Do your partner.
Promenade the set and swing at home.

Allemande Left, then turn your partner by the right.
Allemande Left, then a Grand Right and Left.
Meet your partner, give her a swing and Promenade home.

Gents to the center with a Right-Hand Star.
Then back by the left for a Star Promenade.
Break it all up with a corner swing and Promenade home.

SQUARE DANCE DESCRIPTIONS FOR THE INTERMEDIATE LEVEL

Before going into the figures at the Intermediate Level, it is critical that your group masters the Beginner Level material. Begin your unit with a review and reteaching of all necessary movements, then proceed with the Intermediate Level program. They have been arranged in a progression according to difficulty.

Intermediate Level Characteristics

Characteristics of learners at this level are expanded into three developmental areas: cognitive, affective, and psychomotor. Awareness of these characteristics assists us in selecting chapter content for planning lessons and units. They offer general guidelines, and in the classroom we will each make our final decisions based on specific needs.

Cognitive

- Develop patterns and movement combinations into repeatable sequences.
- Design dance sequences that are personally interesting.
- Recognize the cultural role of dance in understanding others.

Affective

- Appreciate differences and similarities in others' physical activity.
- Respect persons from different backgrounds and the cultural significance of the dances and rhythmic activities.
- Enjoy feelings from involvement in physical activity.

Psychomotor

- Maintain aerobic activity for a specified time.
- Create and perform dances that combine traveling, balancing, and weight transfer with smooth, flowing sequences and intentional changes in direction, speed, and flow.
- Participate vigorously for a sustained time while maintaining a target heart rate.

Intermediate Figures

25. Weave the Ring

A Grand Right and Left without touching hands
Styling: Hands and arms are in a natural position throughout the movement.

26. Pass Through

No hands are used in this movement. Two facing couples walk forward and pass their opposites. They pass right shoulders and remain back-to-back with the other couple to receive the next call (see Figure 6.26).
Styling: Arms in natural position

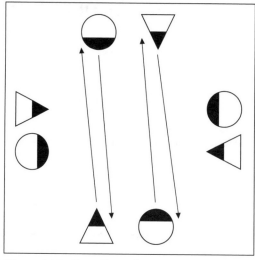

Figure 6.26   Pass Through.

27. Split Outside Couple and Split the Ring

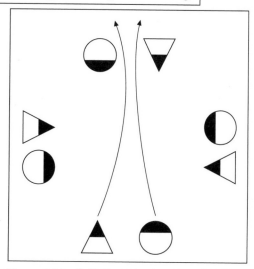

Figure 6.27   Split Outside Couple and Split the Ring.

One couple moves forward to the opposite couple, going through and between them (see Figure 6.27) with the next call indicating the direction to be followed.
Styling: Split the Outside Couple usually involves two couples, and Split the Ring, which is really the same move, may only involve one couple.

28. Rollaway Half Sashay

The girl rolls across a full turn (360 degrees) in front of the boy. The result is that partners have changed places (see Figure 6.28).
Styling: Boy gently pulls the girl across in front of him; she moves to the opposite side as he steps back and to the right.

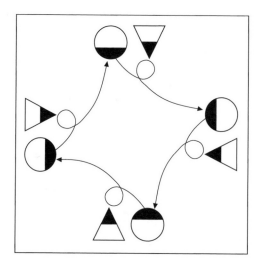

Figure 6.28   Rollaway Half Sashay.

Practice Calls for the Intermediate Level

Do not hurry your students, and allow plenty of time to complete these movements. Use the talk-through, walk-through, dance-through method.

Sample Practice Call

Heads pass through.
Split the couple, around one.
Go into the middle (active couples only).
Form a Right-Hand Star.
Turn it around till your corner comes up.
Left Allemande.

First couple go down the center.
Split the Ring, separate.
Go back home and swing your own.

Couples one and three Pass Through.
Separate, go around two people.
Right back home and swing your own.

Join hands and circle to the left.
All four ladies Rollaway with a Half Sashay.
And keep on circling.

29. U-Turn Back

A single dancer movement with a half turn (180 degrees) (see Figure 6.29). This is a turn in place toward partner unless body flow dictates otherwise.

30. Separate and Divide

Dancers turn back-to-back on a separate, and walk forward around the outside of the square (see Figure 6.30). Follow the next call. On a divide the dancers do the same, but walk only a quarter around the outside of the square.

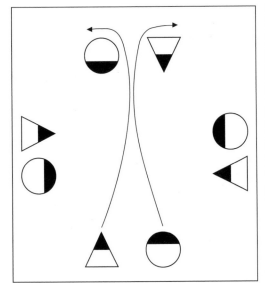

Figure 6.29   U-Turn Back.

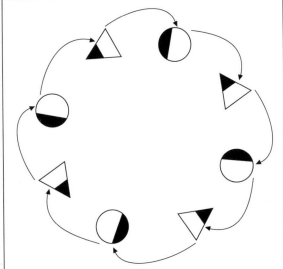

Figure 6.30   Separate and Divide.

31. Wrong Way Grand

Same as the Grand Right and Left, but boys move CW and girls move CCW

32. Courtesy Turn

The boy takes the girl's left hand, palm down in his left hand, which is palm up. He places his right hand in the small of her back. Together they turn until facing center, as the boy backs up and the girl goes forward (see Figure 6.31). She may either hold her skirt or put her free hand on her hip.

center of turn

Figure 6.31 Courtesy Turn.

33. Two or Four Ladies Chain

Two indicated girls extend right hands to each other in the center. They pull by and extend their left hands to the opposite boy, and complete the move with a Courtesy Turn (see Figure 6.32). On the four girls Chain, all four girls go to the center with a Right-Hand Star; turn half around and Courtesy Turn with the opposite boy.

Figure 6.32 Two Ladies Chain.

Sample Practice Call

Couple one (two, three, or four) separate; walk around the set, go back home, and swing your own.

Circle left, then circle to the right.
Boys, U-Turn Back for Left Allemande.

Heads Pass Through and U-Turn Back.
Then Pass Through again and U-Turn Back once more.

Head two girls Chain across the set.
Now the side two girls Chain across the set.
Then all four girls Chain back home.

SQUARE DANCE DESCRIPTIONS FOR THE ADVANCED LEVEL

As they enter this level of square dancing, it is critical that your students have mastery of the preceding figures. Since many students switch schools and teachers at this grade level, allow plenty of time to review and reteach the earlier material. The contents of this section are arranged in a developmental sequence according to difficulty. Mastery of these figures will provide you with some versatile square dancers.

Advanced Level Characteristics

Characteristics of learners at this level are expanded into three developmental areas: cognitive, affective, and psychomotor. Awareness of these characteristics assists us in planning lessons and units. They offer general guidelines, and in the classroom we will each make our final decisions based on specific needs.

Cognitive

- Identify the proper warm-up, conditioning, and cool-down skills and their purposes.
- Describe techniques using body and movement activities to communicate ideas and feelings.
- Describe training and conditioning principles for specific dances and physical activities.

Affective

- Identify, respect, and participate with persons of various skill levels.
- Enjoy aesthetic and creative aspects of performance.
- Respect physical and performance limitations of self and others.
- Enjoy meeting and cooperating with others during physical activity.

Psychomotor

- Perform simple folk, country, and creative dances.
- Sustain aerobic activity, maintaining a target heart rate to achieve cardiovascular benefits.
- Perform dances with fluency and rhythm.
- Participate in dance activities representing various cultural backgrounds.

Advanced Figures

34. Do Paso

Partners face and do a left forearm turn, then a right forearm turn with their corners, and a Courtesy Turn with their partners to face the center of the set or to follow the next call.

35. Lead Right

From a static square or starting formation the designated couple(s) move out to face the couple on their immediate right (see Figure 6.33).
Styling: Inside hands are held in a normal couple hold, and outside hands are in a normal dance position.

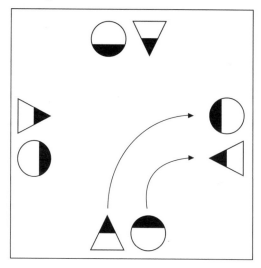

Figure 6.33 Lead Right.

36. Right and Left Through

Two facing couples go toward each other, join right hands, pull by, and give left hands to partners. The movement is completed with a Courtesy Turn. The result is that the couples end up facing across from where they started (see Figure 6.34).

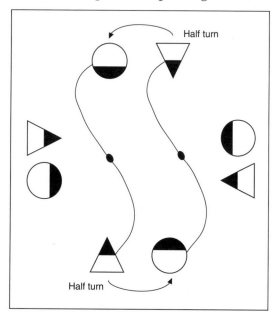

Figure 6.34 Right and Left Through.

37. Star Through

Starting formation is two dancers facing, boy and girl. Boy's right hand is placed against girl's left hand with fingers up to form an arch. The dancers move forward with the girl doing a quarter left face turn under the arch, while the boy does a quarter turn to the right, behind the girl (see Figure 6.35). The dancers end

up side-by-side with the girl on the boy's right.
Styling: hands should be up, palm-to-palm, with enough height for the girl to move comfortably under the arch.

Figure 6.35   Star Through.

38. Circle to a Line

Two facing couples circle left a half turn (180 degrees). The boy indicated by the caller breaks the hold with his left hand, but retains the right-hand hold (see Figure 6.36 a and b). The released dancer moves forward under a raised arm arch (see Figure 6.36c). The dancer becomes the right end in a line of four, facing center. The line straightens out for the next call.

Figure 6.36   Circle to a Line.

39. Bend the Line

A line with an even number of dancers, usually four, all face the same direction and drop hand holds in the center. The ends move forward while the centers back up; both halves of the line are now facing (see Figure 6.37).
Styling: Use normal couple hand holds, and quickly join hands in the new line.

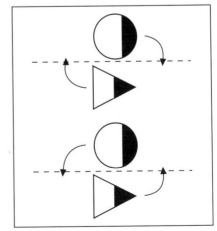

Figure 6.37   Bend the Line.

Practice Calls for the Advanced Level

Remember to use a slow pace and allow plenty of time to complete the figures. However, normal completion time is eight beats of the music.

Girls to the center with a Left-Hand Star.
Back by the right, but not too far.

Meet your partner with a Do Paso.
Turn him by the left and then a right to the corner.
Then Courtesy Turn as you go back home.

Couples one and three do the Right and Left Through.
Couples two and four do the Right and Left Through.
Once again, couples one and three Right and Left Through.

Now two and four do the Right and Left Through.
Allemande Left the corner girl.
Grand Right and Left and Promenade home.

Couples one and three Star Through.
Then Pass Through and Split Two.
Separate and go around one.
Walk down the middle and Star Through again.
Then pass through, Left Allemande. (Repeat for side couples.)

Couples one and three lead to the right.
Head gent break and Circle to a Line.
Go forward and back, then Bend the Line.

Two girls Chain across, then Chain right back.
Allemande Left and Promenade back home.

40. All Around the Left-Hand Lady

Begin with corners facing and walking around each other. Right shoulders are adjacent and remain so throughout the move. Dancers loop in a complete circle to return to face their partners (see Figure 6.38).
Styling: Arms in a natural dance position

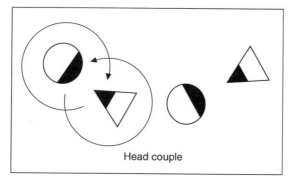

Head couple

Figure 6.38　All Around the Left-Hand Lady.

41. See-Saw (Your Taw)

Start with dancers facing, and in this case partners facing. Following the call, "All around the left-hand girl," move as the above call, walk forward and around your partner keeping left shoulders adjacent throughout the move instead of right shoulders.

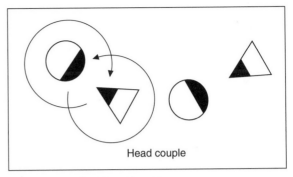

Figure 6.39 See-Saw Your Taw.

42. See-Saw as a Left Shoulder Do-Si-Do

When not used with the call, "All around your left-hand lady," this move is like a Do-Si-Do, except that it starts with left shoulders passing first, instead of right shoulders. When used with the call, "All around your left-hand lady," the moves combine into a flowing figure-8 pattern (see Figure 6.40).

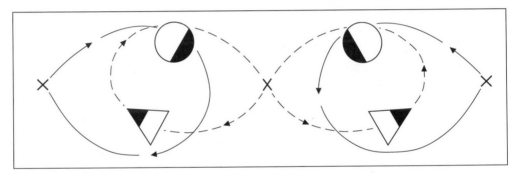

Figure 6.40 All Around and See-Saw combine into a flowing figure-8 pattern.

Sample Practice Call

Heads go forward and back.
Now sides you do the same.
It's all around your left-hand girl.
Then you See-Saw your pretty little taw.

43. Grand Square

The heads and sides perform the movement in different directions (see Figure 6.41 a and b) at the same time on the command, "Sides face, Grand Square." Heads move forward four, turn a quarter on the fourth step to face their partners, and back up four steps. Then they turn a quarter to face their opposites, back up to the corner in four steps, turn a quarter to face partners, and walk home four steps. Do not turn because the action from this point is reversed (total to here is 16 steps or counts). This is the halfway point. Heads now back away from their partners four steps, turning a quarter on the fourth step to face opposites. Then walk forward four, and again on the fourth, step turn a quarter to face the center of the set and your partner. Walk forward four turning a quarter on the fourth step to face opposite, back up four to your home position. This is a 32-count move.

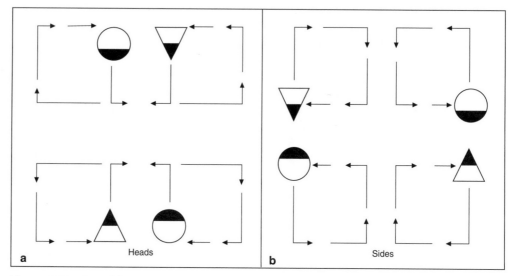

Figure 6.41   Grand Square.

While the heads do their first 16 steps, the sides face their partners to back away and do the second 16 steps. Upon completion of the second 16, the sides do the first 16 steps, while the heads are doing the last 16.

44. Square Through

This may be called for one to five hands. Starts with couples facing, joining right hands and pulling by (see Figure 6.42). Then turn a quarter and join left hands and pull by. A half Square Through has been completed. Turn a quarter again, join right hands and pull by. A three-quarter Square Through has been completed. Turn a quarter more, join left hands and pull by, but do not turn.

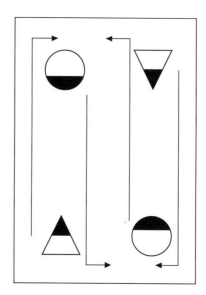

Figure 6.42   Square Through.

Sample Practice Call

Take your time, and don't hurry your students!

Head couples forward and back.
Now forward again with a full Square Through.
Allemande Left with the corner girl.

Couples one and three Square Through.
Split Two go around one to a line of four.
Forward and Back with all eight.
Left Allemande.

Head couples Square Through.
Do-Si-Do the corner and do a Left Allemande.
Come on back with the Right and Left Grand.

Sides face, Grand Square.
Walk, two, three, turn; walk, two, three, turn.
Walk, two, three, turn; walk, two, three, don't turn.
Reverse, two, three, turn; walk, two, three, turn.
Walk, two, three, turn; walk, two, three, you're home.

CLOGGING

Appalachian Clog Dance varies in form from geographic region to region, but it is truly an American folk art. It takes its roots from sources that include England, Ireland, Scotland, and Africa. Our earliest settlers brought these varieties and because of this we cannot identify one source as the true source of clogging. Later, contributions came from Germany and France.

Perhaps clogging arose from the walking step used in Appalachian Big Set as the participants added foot stomping, shuffles, chugs, and heel-toe combinations to emphasize the rhythmic pattern of the music. While a couple waited to dance in the Kentucky Running Set, they would freestyle in place waiting to dance. The men would perform a solo jig called a "hoedown."

Black males added another form of flat-footed chugs and shuffles called the "buck dance." It was this buck dancing that found its way into minstrel shows and vaudeville, and eventually evolved into our modern tap dance and Charleston.

Clogging has continued to grow over the years. It has great appeal because of its relationship to American folk traditions, its exciting rhythms and steps, and its aerobic exercise. Its evolution paralleled that of square dance, both the Big Set and western forms. Depending on the location, the participants might smooth shuffle dance or they might clog dance through the figures. Due to the popularity of clogging while square dancing, a short section on basics is included for you to try in your programs.

Step Description

There are many steps in clogging that have strong regional ties, such as the Western North Carolina Triple, Smoky Mountain Variation, and the Tennessee Walking Step. However, despite all the regional differences, most cloggers share the following basic eight steps in common:

1. Toe

A step or tap on the floor with the ball of the foot

2. Heel

A transfer of weight from the toe to the heel with a snap to make a distinct sound

3. Step

A flat-footed stomp with the heel and toe touching the floor simultaneously

4. Drag (also known as a backward "chug")

The weight on one foot, slide back on that foot, without lifting the toe or heel

5. Slide (also known as a forward chug)

The same as the drag, except forward (similar to a skip)

6. Rock (also known in modern tap as a "step-ball-change")

Step onto the left foot, then place the ball of the right foot slightly behind the left foot. Transfer the weight to the right foot while lifting the left foot. End by stepping again on the left foot. This can also be done starting on the right foot.

7. Brush (also known in modern tap by the same name)

With the weight on one foot, lift the other foot and kick it forward so the ball of the foot brushes the floor (the heel does not sound).

8. Double Toe (also known in modern tap as the "shuffle")

This is a double brush done with your weight on one foot; brush the other foot forward and then back. The knee will straighten slightly on the forward brush and bend slightly on the brush back.

It is from these eight steps that the more complex steps are developed. Steps that include big kicks, knee and foot slaps, heel clicks, and syncopated rhythms, to name a few. The music is usually traditional, reflecting its country, mountain heritage. However, today cloggers are dancing to just about anything.

History

It is felt that the term "clogging" had its roots in the wooden-soled shoes used in old English clog dancing. Today, however, cloggers wear flexible leather-soled shoes and add taps to them to amplify the sound of the steps.

Clogging has moved from the Appalachian Mountains across the United States and has its own national association. It has been included as an alternative to walking through your figures and offers another challenge to add to your square dance program. Since clogging can be done either while square dancing or as a separate activity, these basics will add another colorful dimension to your square dance program.

In addition, it can help develop both physical and social fitness!

SUMMARY

You should now be able to add some variety to your square dance program. Appalachian Big Set serves as a great lead into squares of eight. Clogging to the movements of the dances certainly can add variety to a program. Square Dance forms are developmentally appropriate for your classes. The contents of this chapter have the potential to enliven your classes and have your students wanting more.

CHAPTER 7

FOLK DANCE

Folk dance includes the cultures of many lands. They are brought into this chapter through the dances that pump life and excitement into our programs. There are enough dances in this chapter to keep any teacher active for quite some time.

The chapter begins with an informative description of folk dancing, followed by a sample folk dance lesson plan, and a suggested 15-lesson unit for the second grade. It then moves into the descriptions of the 36 dances that include the basics for a well-rounded, comprehensive unit.

"To Dance is to Live and to Live is to Dance."

(Snoopy)

DESCRIPTION OF FOLK DANCING

Folk dancing is the oldest form of dance and probably one of the earliest forms of communication. It is this self-expression that separates folk dancing from the functional aspects of games and gymnastics in our physical education programs.

Dance is the expression of oneself through rhythmic movement. Folk dance, which is also the expression of oneself, is an expression through patterned movements. It is this patterning that traditionally separates folk dance forms from other dance forms. It is probably this characteristic of folk dance that has turned many youngsters off to dance—their inability to perform a set of patterned movements.

This brings up the argument, discussed in chapter 1, of whether to modify a particular dance for a group. Many say that it is not the proper thing to do, because it destroys the integrity of the dance. It is for this very reason that you may want to have two levels of folk dance for your students. There is a need for a modified level to promote and ensure success, and a need to preserve a dance completely intact for its built-in values. Simplify your dances to raise the success level of students; however, eventually teach your students the prescribed pattern for a given dance. This modification will allow you to bring along all of your students, and eventually allow them to see and perform the complete dance.

Importance of Folk Dancing

Folk dance should be an integral part of all dance programs. The teacher must know when to modify and when to preserve a dance or the students can be lost to dance forever. Knowing what to do at the proper times comes with experience, a willingness to learn, and a desire to promote dance with everyone. It can be any of these three elements or a combination that has caused some teachers to be negative about dance.

Folk dance can be the easiest form of dance to teach. However, not knowing how to modify a dance has probably caused us to turn off young students and perhaps even ourselves. Experiment, simplify, and teach in small segments. Don't be afraid to modify or change the directions to raise success levels.

If we believe that education should be child centered, then folk dance must be modified in the beginning to fit the needs of the student. We must not try to form the student to fit the activity. We all have an obligation to educate youngsters beyond simply movement skills. All children have feelings and thoughts that must be nurtured. We must focus on total development.

When starting dance with children, they need success immediately. Provide activities around basic movements they have done before, and begin focusing on rhythmic movement. Don't even call it dance in the beginning. Be sure to cover all the nonlocomotor, locomotor, and combination movements; then work on phrasing. Youngsters need to internalize phrasing without the pressure of fouling up a patterned dance. Percussion instruments and music can help with this early movement. It is important that contrasts in movement be the focus on this exploration. Contrast is an important element of expression at all levels of dance. If you as a teacher feel more comfortable, it is appropriate to do exercises to music as preparation for dance concepts later. The results of a lesson are important to the teacher, but probably more important to the student. Remember that feelings, creativity, and movement are fundamental to all dance forms.

Starting the Program

Rhythm is the basis of all movement activities, and the key to success hinges on the proper rhythmic execution of any skill. Look for the basic patterns of dance found in nearly every sport. Certainly, these can be useful as lead-ins to your folk dance lessons or any other dance forms.

> 'The true dance must have soul, express passion, and imitate nature!' Writers in the late 1800s sing the praises of folk dances, which to them barely veil the wooing of the sexes in rhythmical movements, express passion, and imitate a small part of human nature. (Sachs, 1937, p. 429)

> For that to which they give living expression has been the secret longing of man from the very beginning—the victory over gravity, over all that weighs down and oppresses, the change of body into spirit, the elevation of creature into creator, the merging with the infinite, the divine. 'Whosoever knoweth the power of the dance dwelleth in God.' (Sachs, 1937, p. 448)

The following selection provides a wide variety of folk dances from which to choose. This allows you maximum flexibility in meeting your programmatic needs. There is plenty here for everyone.

Each dance begins with a description, record listing, and formation to simplify starting and teaching. Although all the dances are relatively easy, they are arranged in three groups. This organization will assist the beginning teacher in starting with the easiest dances to ensure success for both students and teachers.

LIST OF FOLK DANCES IN THIS CHAPTER

The following list contains the name of each dance in its order in the book. Following this list is a description of the dances.

FOLK DANCE DESCRIPTIONS FOR THE BEGINNER LEVEL

The folk dances for this level introduce various cultures and movements that can bring this process to life for your students.

Beginner Level Characteristics

Characteristics of learners at this level are expanded into three developmental areas: cognitive, affective, and psychomotor. Awareness of these characteristics assists us in planning lessons and units. They offer general guidelines, and in the classroom we will each make our final decisions based on specific needs.

Cognitive

- Recognize that movement concepts are similar in a variety of skills.
- Identify appropriate behaviors in physical activities for participating with others.

Affective

- Enjoy participation alone and with others.
- Appreciate the benefits that accompany cooperation and sharing.
- Show consideration toward others in the physical activity setting.

Psychomotor

- Travel in different ways in a large group without bumping into others or falling.
- Distinguish among straight, curved, and zigzag pathways while traveling in various ways.
- Combine various traveling patterns in time to the music.
- Skip, hop, gallop, and slide using mature motor patterns.

1. Hokey Pokey

Description: An American nonpartner dance for all ages

Music: Old Timer Record No. 8086.

Formation: Single circle, partnerless, and facing center

Counts and Steps:

PART A:

1-4—In a circle, all may sing. Verse 1: "You put your right hand in," and all right hands extend to the center of the circle.

5-8—"You take your right hand out."

1-8—"You put your right hand in and you shake it all about."

PART B:

1-16—"Then you do the Hokey Pokey and you turn yourself about. That's what it's all about!"

After shaking the "right hand all about" everyone holds up arms and turns around in four counts and then faces anyone nearby. When the song says, "That's what it's all about," everyone slaps thighs twice, claps own hands twice, and then claps hands with the other person three times. Repeat this process with the following verses:

Verse 2: Left hand
Verse 3: Right foot
Verse 4: Left foot
Verse 5: Right elbow
Verse 6: Left elbow
Verse 7: Whole self
Verse 8: Head
Verse 9: Backside
Verse 10: Hokey Pokey—As the first Hokey Pokey comes, bend down and straighten up again while singing. Do it again on the second count. On the third, kneel down on hands and knees, and pound on the floor. Stand up again on the last count.

2. Amos Moses (Hully Gully)

Description: An American novelty nonpartner eight-count dance

Music: Jerry Reed, "Amos Moses," RCA, 0896 or 9904.

Formation: No partners, stand anywhere on floor, face front

Counts and Steps:

1-2—Right heel forward and close.

3-4—Left heel forward and close.

5—Step forward on right.

6—Step left foot behind right foot.

7—Step forward on right foot with a quarter turn right.

8—Step forward on left foot and close beside right.

Repeat until record ends.

3. Carnavalito

Description: This is a Bolivian festival dance done primarily at carnival time, hence the name, Carnavalito.

Music: #11352 available from The Folk Dancer Record Service, Box 2305, N. Babylon, NY 11702.

Formation: Circle, broken circle, or lines (the line may be an "S" formation); hands joined, with bodies a quarter turn to right, facing leader

Counts and Steps:

PART A:

1-4—Four steps forward, starting with right foot; bend forward and hold. Try this in an "S" formation.

5-8—Four steps forward, starting with left foot; bend forward and hold.

1-8—Repeat steps for first set of counts 1 to 8.

PART B:

1-16—Change the forward steps to step-hops. Leader pulls line into a big circle with 16 step-hops.

1-16—Circle reverses as person at the opposite end pulls the line for 16 step-hops.

Reverse direction and start from beginning.

4. Danish Dance of Greeting

Description: Danish circle dance for couples

Music: Folkcraft, 1187 x 45 B.

Formation: Single circle of couples, facing center

Cues:

Clap, clap, bow,
Clap, clap, bow,
Stamp, stamp,
Turn yourself around.

Counts and Steps:

PART A:

1-2—Clap hands twice and bow to partner on counts 1 and 2.

3-4—Clap hands twice and bow to neighbor on counts 3 and 4.

5-6—Stamp twice in place, facing center on counts 5 and 6.

7-8—Turn once in place with four running steps on counts 7 and 8.

1-8—Repeat steps for first set of counts 1 to 8.

PART B:

1-16—All join hands and circle to the left with 16 light running steps.

PART C:

1-16—Circle right with 16 light running steps.

5. German Wedding Dance

Description: This is a German wedding dance.

Music: Waltz or Polka

Formation: Boys in one line face girls in another; dancers move to top of set when their turns come up.

Counts and Steps: There are no specific counts for this dance.

Head couples form an arch with inside hands.

Walk down the girl's line (see Figure 7.1) and up the boy's line.

Drop hands and boy chases girl to the bottom of the set.

New head couples repeat the dance.

Figure 7.1   German Wedding Dance.

6. Chimes of Dunkirk

Description: French-Belgian circle dance for couples

Music: Folkcraft, 1188 x 45.

Formation: Single circle of couples, partners facing

Counts and Steps:

PART A:

1-4—Three stamps in place beginning on the left foot, count 1, 2, 3 pause.

5-8—Clap hands three times, count 1, 2, 3 pause.

PART B:

1-8—Join both hands with partner and turn clockwise (CW) once around with eight running steps, and bow.

PART C:

1-16—All join hands and circle left with 16 running steps; end with a bow.

7. Kinderpolka

Description: A German dance

Music: Folkdance Funfest, Educational Recordings of America, #XTV 69269.

Formation: Partners in a single circle, girl on boy's right, face each other, join both hands and extend them sideward at shoulder height.

Counts and Steps:

PART A:

1-2—Take two sideward steps to center, begin on boy's left, girl's right; step-close, step-close on counts 1 and 2 and.

3-4—Stamp lightly three times, with boy's left, girl's right on counts 3 and 4.

5-6—Take two sideward steps away from center; step-close, step-close on counts 5 and 6.

7-8—Stamp-stamp-stamp on counts 7 and 8.

1-8—Repeat steps for first set of counts 1 to 8.

PART B:

1-4—Partners face and clap own knees one time, own hands one time, then partner's hands three times. The count is 1 clap knees, 2 clap hands, 3 and 4 clap partner's hands three times.

5-8—Repeat the steps for counts 1 to 4.

PART C:

1-2—Spring lightly in place on left foot; place right heel forward, toe up, and shake right forefinger at partner, "scolding" on counts 1 and 2.

3-4—Do same with left heel and left forefinger on counts 3 and 4.

5-8—Turn around in place with four steps, face partner, and stamp three times on counts 5, 6, 7, and 8.

8. Jump Jim Jo

Description: This is an American couple dance that contains the progression of partner exchange.

Music: *First Folk Dances*, RCA, LPM 1625.

Formation: Couples in a circle with boy's back to center of the circle; both hands are joined.

Words:

> "Jump, jump, oh jump, Jim Jo,
> Take a little whirl, and around you go,
> Slide, slide and stamp just so,
> You're a sprightly little fellow
> When you jump, Jim Jo."

Alternate words for the last two lines are:

> "Then you take another partner
> And you jump, Jim Jo."

Words, Counts, and Steps:

"Jump, jump, oh jump, Jim Jo"

1-4—Dancers jump to the side in a counterclockwise (CCW) direction with two slow jumps, followed by three quick jumps in place, counts 1, 2, 3, and 4.

"Take a little whirl, and around you go"

5-8—Drop hands to sides, each turns in place to the right, with four slow jumps, once around, counts 5, 6, 7, and 8.

(**Alternate version:** Boy twirls the girl under joined right hands.)

"Slide, slide and stamp just so"

1-4—Couples rejoin hands and slide slowly CCW twice, then stamp feet three times, counts 1, 2, 3, and 4.

"Then you take another partner, and you jump, Jim Jo"

5-8—Each dancer moves right with four light running steps, and then jumps quickly, three times, counts 5, 6, 7, and 8.

Repeat dance from beginning with new partner.

Variation: Instead of the two slow slides in a CCW direction, couples may run around in place with a two-hand hold and stay with the same partner for the three quick jumps.

9. La Candeliere

Description: This Italian wedding dance is also known as "The Candle Dance."

Music: Waltz or Polka

Formation: Two lines, boys face girls in other line; dancers move to top of set when their turns come up. Two boys and one girl stand at head facing down the center.

Counts and Steps: There are no specific counts in this dance.

Girl gives the candle to one of the boys and dances down the center to the bottom of the set with the other boy.

Two new girls come in and the boy gives candle to one and dances with other. Repeat these patterns over and over.

Can use a bouquet of flowers instead of a candle.

10. Carousel

Description: This is a Danish couple dance.

Music: Folkdance Funfest, Educational Recordings of America, #XTV 69269.

Formation: Double circle of couples face center. Girls join hands in center of circle; boys behind them. Place both hands on partners' shoulders.

Counts and Steps:

PART A:

1-16—All take 16 slow sliding steps to left, CW.

1-16—As music speeds up, take 16 fast sliding steps to left.

PART B:

1-16—Take 16 fast sliding steps to right, CCW.

1-16—Take 16 fast sliding steps to right and at end, boys quickly change places with girls. Now boys are in front; and repeat dance from beginning.

11. Shoemaker's Dance

Description: This is a Danish couple dance.

Music: Folkcraft, 1187 x 45 A.

Formation: Double circle, partners facing

Counts and Steps:

PART A:

Cues:

Wind, wind, wind the bobbin, wind, wind, wind the bobbin,
Wind, wind, wind the bobbin, wind, wind, wind the bobbin,
Pull, pull, pull, pull, clap, clap, clap, or tap, tap, tap.

1-2—With arms bent at shoulder height and hands clenched to form fists, circle one fist over the other in front of chest, "winding the bobbin," counts 1 and 2 and.

3-4—Reverse circle and "wind" in opposite direction, counts 3 and 4 and.

5-6—Pull elbows back vigorously twice, "pulling and tightening the thread," counts 5 and 6.

7-8—Clap own hands three times, counts 7 and 8.

1-8—Repeat the steps for first set of counts 1 to 8.

PART B:

1-16—Partners face CCW with inside hands joined. Skip 16 times forward, ending with a bow on the last count.

Repeat the dance.

Variation: In this variation dancers move their feet more than in the first version. This version requires the dancers to have a little more coordination.

PART A:

1-2—Place heel of outside foot forward.

3-4—Point toe of outside foot in back.

5-8—Three running steps forward; start with outside foot and pause.

1-8—Repeat pattern for first set of counts 1 to 8, starting with inside foot.

PART B:

1-16—Repeat steps for first two sets of counts 1 to 8.

Song for Above Variation:

> Heel and toe and away we go,
> Heel and toe and away we go,
> See my new shoes neatly done,
> Away we go to have some fun.

12. Seven Jumps

Description: This Danish dance was originally danced by men only. Any number of people may participate. Dancers must hold position for the duration of the note.

Music: *All Purpose Folk Dances*, RCA, LPM 1623.

Formation: Single circle, all hands joined. The dance may be done as a couple formation, with partners joining both hands for the Chorus and facing each other for the figures.

Counts and Steps:

PART A:

1-16—Chorus: Begin the dance with the Chorus and return to it after each of the seven figures below. Chorus consists of seven step-hops to the left with a jump on the eighth count.

1-16—Repeat step-hops and jump to the right. Step-hop by stepping, then hopping on one foot as the opposite leg swings forward and across. The jump may be left out for general use, and dancers may instead do eight step-hops to the left, then eight to the right.

Seven figures: Stand motionless only on the last sustained note of music in each figure.

PART B:

1—Figure 1, right foot—On first sustained note, place hands on hips and raise right knee. Do not lower knee until the second note, and stand motionless throughout the third note.

2-32—Repeat Chorus with the steps for both sets of counts 1 to 16 in Part A.

PART C:

1-2—Figure 2, left foot—Repeat Figure 1, and add identical figure with left knee.

3-32—Repeat Chorus with the steps for both sets of counts 1 to 16 in Part A.

PART D:

1-3—Figure 3, right knee—Repeat Figures 1 and 2, and kneel on right knee.

4-32—Repeat Chorus with the steps for both sets of counts 1 to 16 in Part A.

PART E:

1-4—Figure 4, left knee—Repeat Figures 1, 2, 3, and kneel on left knee.

5-32—Repeat Chorus with the steps for both sets of counts 1 to 16 in Part A.

PART F:

1-5—Figure 5, right elbow—Repeat Figures 1, 2, 3, 4, and place right elbow on floor.

6-32—Repeat Chorus with the steps for both sets of counts 1 to 16 in Part A.

PART G:

1-6—Figure 6, left elbow—Repeat Figures 1, 2, 3, 4, 5, and place left elbow on floor.

7-32—Repeat Chorus with the steps for both sets of counts 1 to 16 in Part A.

PART H:

1-7—Figure 7, head—Repeat Figures 1, 2, 3, 4, 5, 6, and place head on floor.

8-32—Finish dance with a final Chorus.

FOLK DANCE DESCRIPTIONS FOR THE INTERMEDIATE LEVEL

These folk dances are a fun way to teach students to respect those from different backgrounds.

Intermediate Level Characteristics

Characteristics of learners at this level are expanded into three developmental areas: cognitive, affective, and psychomotor. Awareness of these characteristics assists us in planning lessons and units. They offer general guidelines, and in the classroom we will each make our final decisions based on specific needs.

Cognitive

- Develop patterns and movement combinations into repeatable sequences.
- Design dance sequences that are personally interesting.
- Recognize the cultural role of dance in understanding others.

Affective

- Appreciate differences and similarities in others' physical activity.
- Respect persons from different backgrounds and the cultural significance of the dances and rhythmic activities.
- Enjoy feelings from involvement in physical activity.

Psychomotor

- Maintain aerobic activity for a specified time.

- Create and perform dances that combine traveling, balancing, and weight transfer with smooth sequences and intentional changes in direction, speed, and flow.
- Participate vigorously for a sustained time while maintaining a target heart rate.

13. Bunny Hop

Description: An American conga-style dance for all ages

Music: Macgregor Records, #6995-B.

Formation: Single line, single file, hands on hips of person in front of you. You may wish to alternate boy, girl, using either boy or girl at head of line (see Figure 7.2).

Figure 7.2 Single-file formation for the Bunny Hop.

Counts and Steps:

1-4—Start with both feet together, put left foot out to the side and back, two times; out, back, out, back.

5-8—Then put right foot out and back to the side, two times; out, back, out, back.

5—Jump forward once, count 5.

6—Jump backward once, count 6.

7-8—Jump forward three times, counts 7-and-8.

Repeat the dance.

14. Ten Pretty Girls

Description: This American dance does not require partners and can be done in many forms. It is appealing to any age group. It is said to have originated in Texas, but no proof has been found.

Music: Folk Dance for Fun, #LPM 1624.

Formation: Any number of dancers, side-by-side in a circle or in lines. They may hold hands or place hands behind each other's backs.

Counts and Steps:

PART A:

1—Start on right foot, place right toe forward and pause, count 1.

2—Place right toe to the right side and pause, count 2.

3-4—Take three steps, moving sideward to the left, right foot, left foot, right foot. Step on the right in back of the left while moving sideward on the first count, counts 3 and 4.

5—Place left toe forward and pause, count 5.

6—Place left toe sideward to the left and pause, count 6.

7-8—Take three quick steps moving sideward to the right; left foot, right foot, left foot. The first step on the left foot is taken in back of right foot, counts 7 and 8.

PART B:

1-4—All move forward four steps, strutting; right foot, left foot, right foot, left foot.

5—Vigorously kick right foot forward and lean body back.

6—Vigorously kick right foot backward and lean body forward. Make a half turn facing the opposite direction.

7-8—Stamp feet in place lightly three times; right foot, left foot, right foot. Repeat dance from beginning. Start with the left foot and end with the left foot swinging forward and back.

The dance is repeated, starting with the other foot each time.

15. Skip to My Lou

Description: An American circle dance

Music: *Sing and Dance*, Educational Recordings of America, XTV 69283.

Formation: Single circle, couples with inside hands joined, facing LOD (line of direction)

Counts and Steps:

PART A:

1-16—"Skip, skip, skip to my Lou, skip, skip, skip to my Lou, skip, skip, skip to my Lou, skip to my Lou, my darling." While singing, couples join inside hands, 16 skips CCW in a circle.

PART B:

1-16—"Lost my true love, what'll I do, lost my true love, what'll I do, lost my true love, what'll I do, skip to my Lou, my darling." While singing, boys make a half turn around and 16 skips CW. Girls continue with 16 skips CCW.

PART C:

1-16—"Found another one, prettier'n you, found another one, prettier'n you, found another one, prettier'n you, skip to my Lou, my darling." While singing, each boy finds a new partner and swings her with a two-hand skipping swing in place. He puts her on his right side and repeats the dance. Those without partners go to the center of circle for "lost and found," find a partner, and join circle.

16. Bleking

Description: This is a Swedish couple dance.

Music: Folkcraft, 1188 x 45 B.

Formation: Double circle, partners facing, arms extended forward at shoulder height, both hands joined with partner

Counts and Steps:

PART A:

1-2—Bleking step is hop on left foot and place right heel forward, thrusting right arm forward and pulling left elbow back vigorously; a slight jump onto right foot placing left heel forward, thrusting left arm forward and pulling right elbow back vigorously, counts 1 and 2.

3-4—Repeat the steps in counts 1 and 2 in double time making three quick changes, alternating right heel, left heel, right heel forward, counts 3 and 4.

5-8—Repeat the steps in counts 1 to 4, reversing footwork and armwork, counts 5, 6, 7, and 8.

1-8—Repeat the steps in the first set of counts 1 to 8. Finish facing partner, both arms extended sideward with hands joined.

PART B:

1-8—Turn CW with partner with eight step-hops; move arms down and up windmill fashion with each step-hop.

1-8—Turn CCW with partner and do eight step-hops in the same manner.

17. La Raspa

Description: La Raspa is a novelty dance, rather than one of Mexico's traditional dances. In the United States it is quite often called the Mexican Hat Dance.

Music: Folkcraft Records, F 111 9 A.

Formation: Couples scattered around the room, partners facing each other

Counts and Steps:

PART A: CHORUS

1-4—Hold two hands. Hop on left foot and send right foot forward, heel down, toe up. Hop on left foot and send right foot forward, heel down, toe up, counts 1, 2, 3, and 4; clap, clap.

5-8—Repeat above, starting on right foot. Repeat again starting on left foot. Repeat again starting on right foot, counts 5, 6, 7, and 8; clap, clap.

Repeat the above 3 times.

PART B:

1-8—Clap hands once, hook right elbows with partner and skip around eight steps.

1-8—Clap hands again, hook left elbows and skip around eight steps.

1-16—Repeat steps for both sets of 1 to 8 counts.

Repeat the dance from beginning.

Part B, variation 1:

1-32—Skip 16 steps linking right elbows, and 16 linking left elbows. Do not repeat.

Part B, variation 2:

1-32—Take ballroom position and do a Polka around the ring for 16 Polka steps.

Part B, variation 3:

1-32—Face partner (all should be in a single-circle formation for this version), and do a Grand Right and Left around the circle. At the end of the chorus take a new partner and repeat the dance from the beginning.

18. Red River Valley

Description: American folk dance in groups of three

Music: Folkcraft Records, 1269 x 45 B.

Formation: Circling in sets of six that break to two facing lines of three dancers, trios are formed by one boy and two girls, or one girl and two boys. Join hands in lines of three. All sing lustily while dancing the action indicated in words of song.

Song:

Oh, you lead right down in the valley
And you circle to the left, go once around
Now you swing with the girl in the valley
And you swing with your Red River Gal.

Oh, you lead right down in the valley
And you circle to the left and to the right
Now the girls Star Right in the valley
And the boys Do-Si-Do so polite.

Oh, you lead right down in the valley
And you circle to the left and to the right
Now you lose your girl in the valley
And you lose your Red River Gal.

Counts and Steps:

PART A:

1-8—Lines of three walk forward bearing right, passing opposite set, to meet a new line of three.

1-8—Join hands with new set to form a circle of six. Walk four steps to the left, then four steps to the right.

1-8—Center dancer in each set swings left-hand dancer.

PART B:

1-16—Repeat steps in first two sets of 1 to 8 in Part A.

1-8—Four girls join right hands across in center to form a right-hand star. Walk CW once around; drop back to place on last two counts to clear the way for the boys' Do-Si-Do.

1-8—The two center dancers Do-Si-Do.

PART C:

1-16—Repeat the steps for first two sets of counts 1 to 8 in Part A.

1-8—The two dancers on the right of this three-person line, the right-hand partners, change places by passing right shoulders diagonally across the set.

1-8—The two dancers on the left of this three-person line, the left-hand partners, change places by passing right shoulders diagonally across the set.

Repeat entire dance with new partners each time.

19. Salty Dog Rag

Description: This is an American couple or line dance that is very popular in folk dance groups.

Music: MCA Records, MCA-60090 (81745).

Formation: Couples side-by-side, skaters' position

Counts and Steps:

PART A:

1-8—Schottische right foot, left foot, right foot, and hop; left foot, right foot, left foot, and hop, to the right side and return.

1-8—Four step-hops forward.

1-8—Repeat the steps in the first set of counts 1 to 8.

1-8—Repeat the steps in the second set of counts 1 to 8.

PART B:

1-8—Face partner and hold hands. Schottische right and left as in the first set of counts 1 to 8 in Part A.

1-8—Holding right hands, do four step-hops in a circle CW.

1-8—Face partner and hold hands. Schottische right and left as in the first set of counts 1 to 8 in Part A.

1-8—Holding left hands, do four step-hops in a circle CCW.

Repeat the dance.

Line Dance Modification:

PART A:

1-8—Schottische right and left.

1-8—Four step-hops in place.

1-8—Schottische right and left.

1-8—Four step-hops in place.

PART B:

1-16—Forward four steps and backward four steps, two times.

1-16—Right heel forward, close, left heel forward, close, right heel forward, close; clap, clap, clap.

Repeat the dance.

20. Solomon Levi

Description: This is a four-couple circle American folk dance. Sing during this dance.

Music: Shaw, 501/502.

Formation: Four couples holding inside hands

Counts and Steps:

PART A:

1-8—First couple separate, go around the outside track.

1-8—Pass your partner over there, pass her coming back.

PART B:

1-8—Bow to your corner; bow to the partners all.

1-8—Swing your partner round and round and Promenade the hall.

PART C:

1-8—Hey Solomon Levi, La La La La La.

1-8—Oh Solomon Levi, La La La La La.

Note: The tune plays through nine times. Add variety by having the heads, sides, and all four do the figure at the same time, or repeat for each couple.

21. Sally Good'in

Description: A four-couple circle American folk dance

Music: Dances from *Appalachia Album*, Berea College Christmas Dance School, CPO 287, Berea, KY 40404.

Formation: Four-couple circle, each couple holding inside hands

PART A:

1-8—First boy out and swing Sally Good'in.

Boy 1 swings right-hand girl Sally Good'in with right arm around.

1-8—Now your Taw.

Boy 1 swings own partner left arm around.

1-8—Swing that girl from Arkansas.

Boy 1 swings opposite girl (Arkansas) with right arm around.

1-8—Then swing Sally Good'in.

Boy 1 swings Sally Good'in with left arm around.

PART B:

1-8—And now your Taw.

Boy 1 swings own partner right arm around.

1-8—Now don't forget your old Grandma.

Boy 1 swings corner girl (Grandma) with left arm around.

1-16—Home you go and everybody swing. Swing with waist swings.

Repeat the steps in Parts A and B with boys 1 and 2 leading out and doing figure simultaneously.

Repeat the steps in Parts A and B again with boys 1, 2, and 3 leading out and dancing the figure simultaneously.

Repeat the steps in Parts A and B the fourth time; all four boys leading out and dancing the figure simultaneously.

22. The Irish Washerwoman

Description: A four-couple circle Irish-American folk dance

Music: *All Purpose Folk Dances*, RCA, LPM 1623.

Formation: Circles of four couples, girls on the right, all facing center, couples holding inside hands

Counts and Steps:

"All four boys to the right of the ring
And when you get there you balance and swing."

1-8—Boys step behind their own partners and to the next girl on the right. Balance and swing once around in place so that the new partners are on boys' right.

"Now Allemande Left with your corners all
And Grand Right and Left around the hall."

1-8—Facing Corners, all Allemande Left and move directly into the next portion of the call.

1-16—The Grand Right and Left is a natural extension of the Allemande Left. Continue until boys meet new partners.

Repeat dance from the beginning as often as desired or until boys meet original partners in a final "Grand Right and Left."

Variations: The first call can be, "Four girls to the right," instead of "boys." Instead of a Grand Right and Left, the call can be, "and Promenade around the hall." After an Allemande Left with the Corners, all Promenade with partners around the circle and back to home position.

A possible introduction before the first call can be: "Into the center and everyone shout! Back to your places and circle about." All join hands, skip to the center and shout, back to place, and circle left until reaching original position.

23. Gustaf's Skoal

Description: This is a Swedish four-couple dance.

Music: Folkdance Funfest, Educational Recordings of America, #XTV 69270.

Formation: Circles of four couples as in American circle dancing, facing center, inside hands joined

Counts and Steps:

PART A:

1-4—Head couples one and three, with inside hands joined, walk forward four steps, bowing deeply on fourth.

5-8—Walk four steps backward to place.

1-8—Side couples repeat steps in counts 1 to 8.

1-8—Head couples repeat steps in the first set of counts 1 to 8.

1-8—Side couples repeat steps in the first set of counts 1 to 8.

PART B:

1-8—As side couples raise partners' joined hands to make arches, head couples skip forward.

1-8—Separate and go under the arch and return to place.

1-8—Join hands with partners and swing with skipping steps.

1-8—Sides do same action as head couples making arches.

FOLK DANCE DESCRIPTIONS FOR THE ADVANCED LEVEL

The advanced level folk dances are a great place to integrate social studies and enjoy cultural differences. It is a time to challenge students and take them to new levels in their personal quests for learning.

Advanced Level Characteristics

Characteristics of learners at this level are expanded into three developmental areas: cognitive, affective, and psychomotor. Awareness of these characteristics assists us in planning lessons and units. They offer general guidelines, and in the classroom we will each make our final decisions based on specific needs.

Cognitive

- Identify the proper warm-up, conditioning, and cool-down skills and their purposes.
- Describe techniques using body and movement activities to communicate ideas and feelings.
- Describe training and conditioning principles for specific dances and physical activities.

Affective

- Identify, respect, and participate with persons of various skill levels.
- Enjoy the aesthetic and creative aspects of performance.
- Respect physical and performance limitations of self and others.
- Enjoy meeting and cooperating with others during physical activity.

Psychomotor

- Perform simple folk, country, and creative dances.
- Sustain aerobic activity, maintaining a target heart rate to achieve cardiovascular benefits.
- Perform dances with fluency and rhythm.
- Participate in dance activities representing various cultural backgrounds.

24. Biserka

Description: A Serbian dance for closing an evening

Music: Folkcraft, 1567 x 45 A.

Formation: Single circle facing LOD, hold hands with person on either side forming the circle.

Counts and Steps:

1-2—Step right CCW with right foot and then left foot.

3-4—Two-step forward (right foot, left foot, right foot).

5-6—Face center; balance in on left foot and back on right foot.

7-8—Two-step moving CW (left foot, right foot, left foot).

Repeat the dance.

25. Bummel Schottische

Description: This dance originated in Mecklenburg, Germany. The following words were usually sung with the movements:

Mother Wittsch, Mother Wittsch, just look at me!
How well I dance just look and see!
First on my heels, then on my toes,
O Mother Wittsch, how well it goes.
Chorus: Tra-la-la and so on.

Music: *Folk Dances from Around the World*, Rhythms Productions, Vol. 1, Side A, #CC 601-1.

Formation: Couples are in sweetheart position, girl in front of boy, hands raised to shoulders, palms forward. Boy, standing behind, takes her hands in his.

PART A:

1-4—Left heel and toe, step, close, step, hop 1, 2, 3, and 4.

5-8—Right heel and toe, step, close, step, hop 5, 6, 7, and 8.

Repeat the steps for counts 1 to 8. When moving to the right the second time, the girl turns out to the right to face her partner in a shoulder-waist position.

PART B:

1-16—Dance the Schottische around the room left-right-left-hop, right-left-right-hop, step-hop, step-hop, step-hop, step-hop.

Repeat the steps for first set of counts 1 to 16.

26. Hora (Hava Nagila)

Description: The Hora may be the national dance of Israel. The Hora step is the basic step of dances in such countries as Greece, Romania, Bulgaria, and Yugoslavia. It is, therefore, a dance that all folk dancers should learn. There is an Old and a New Hora. The New Hora, as done in Israel, is more energetic, with dancers springing high in the air and whirling around with shouts of ecstasy. This record can be used for either version. There are many tunes to which the Hora is done, but the melody of "Hava Nagila" is the favorite.

Music: *All Purpose Folk Dances*, RCA, LPM 1623.

Formation: A circle of dancers, no partners, hands on each other's shoulders

Counts and Steps:

OLD HORA:

1-6—Step to left on left foot. Cross right foot in back of left, with weight on right. Step to left on left foot and hop on it, swinging right foot forward. Step-hop on right foot and swing left foot forward.

This step is repeated over and over. The circle may also move to the right, in which case the same step is used, but beginning with the right foot.

NEW HORA:

1-6—Face a little to the left, count 1 and run two steps, counts 1, 2, left, right. Jump on both feet close together, count 3, hop on left foot, count 4, swing right foot forward. Take three quick steps in place, right, left, right, counts 5 and 6. Count 1, 2, 3, 4, 5, and 6.

Continue in same manner, moving always to left.

If circle moves to right, do same steps but start on right foot.

The dance often begins with the dancers swaying in place from left to right, as music builds up. The dance gradually increases in place and intensity. Shouts accompany the dance as dancers call to each other across the circle. The title, Hava Nagila, means "Come, let us be gay."

27. Virginia Reel

Description: This is an American contra dance that came to us from England and was originally known as Sir Roger de Coverly.

Probably the most popular of the contra or "longway" dances, the Virginia Reel is usually done in family style with all participants active throughout. It is done to many tunes; this recording uses a medley of familiar tunes to encourage group singing in Part C.

Music: *All Purpose Folk Dances*, RCA, LPM 1623.

Formation: A longways set of six couples—two parallel facing lines, all ladies on the left and all gents on the right from the head couple.

Counts and Steps:

PART A:

1-8—"Forward and back" Both lines take four steps to center, bow to partner and four steps back to place.

1-8—"Right hand around" Partners meet, join right hands, swing once around, CW, and return to place.

1-8—"Left hand around" Repeat, using left hand and swinging CCW.

1-8—"Both hands around" Repeat using both hands and turning CW.

PART B:

The counts depend on the number in the set.

"Head couple down and back" Head couple joins both hands and Sashays down the set and back to head position. Sashay with quick, but smooth, sliding side-steps.

"Reel the set" Head couple hooks right elbows, turns once and a half around, then separates and goes to opposite line. Head boy turns second girl once around with a left elbow turn, as head girl does the same with the second boy.

Head couple meets in center for a right elbow turn and continues to the third girl and boy for a left elbow turn.

Head couple continues down the set in this fashion. Left elbow turns to the set, right elbow turns in the center until it has "reeled" the entire set.

At the foot of the set, head couple swings halfway around so the boy and girl are on correct side, joins hands, and Sashays back to places.

PART C:

"Cast off to the foot" To the foot of the line, head couple leads to the outside. Boy to his left, girl to her right, and followed by the lines, the couple marches to the foot of the set.

"Form the arch" Upon reaching the foot of the set, head couple joins hands to form an arch. The others, now led by the second couple, join hands and Sashay through the arch. Second couple leads to the head of the set where it now stands as head couple for the next figure.

When all couples have gone through the arch, head couple drops hands and steps back to become the foot couple.

In this manner, after six changes, each couple will have had its turn as head couple.

28. Winston-Salem Partner Dance

Description: This is a fun American partner dance with many smooth-flowing figures that came from the Southern District AAHPERD Convention when it was held in Winston-Salem, NC.

Music: B.J. Thomas, "Whatever Happened to Old Fashioned Love."

Formation: Couples scattered in the room, partners side-by-side holding inside hands

Counts and Steps:

1-8—Begin with the outside foot. Boys place left heel out at a diagonal; girls place right heel out at a diagonal; and close. Repeat on the inside foot. Repeat from beginning.

1-8—Balance away and together two times or a step-ball-change, step-ball-change.

1-4—Face each other and Grapevine to boy's left for four steps.

5-8—Full turn back to place for four steps to closed position.

1-8—Four two-steps for a full turn.

Repeat the dance.

Variation: This can be done as a mixer with one circle. Boys move forward, CCW during the two-step turn to next girl on the circle.

29. Scandinavian Polka

Description: A couple dance using parts of the Polka step

Music: Any Polka, but not too fast.

Formation: Couples start facing each other, holding hands, scattered around the room; girl does opposite footwork.

Counts and Steps:

1-4—Step left foot, right foot, left foot, and kick right foot.

5-8—Turn back in the opposite direction, right, left, right, kick.

1-4—Four steps with full turn beginning on left foot, right foot, left foot, and right foot. Boy's hands on girl's waist and girl's hands on boy's shoulders moving CW.

30. Miserlou

Description: This is a Greek-American line dance, no partners; Miserlou is a girl's name that means "beloved." The dance utilizes typical Greek steps, and it was popularized by the dancers at Duquesne University in Pittsburgh, PA.

Music: Folkcraft, 1060 x 45 A.

Formation: Open or broken circle, or line has no partners, leader at right end, "W" shape. Elbows bent, hands joined (right holding neighbor's left), resembling the letter "W." Right foot is free (see Figure 7.3).

Figure 7.3 Open or broken circle formation for the Miserlou.

Counts and Steps:

1-4—Step sideward right on right foot, pause. Point left toe across in front of right foot, pause.

5-8—Swing left leg around in an outward arc to cross and step on left foot in back of right. Step sideward right on right foot cross and step on left foot in front of right foot. Pivot on ball of left foot to face slightly left; swing right leg around in front.

1-4—Facing slightly left and moving that direction, one two-step right forward; raise right heel, bending left knee slightly.

5-8—Two-step left backward, pivot on ball of left foot to face center.

31. Farmer's Jig

Description: This is an English contra dance.

Music: *Barn Dance Two*, EFDSS Records, BR2, XGR17.

Formation: Longways set for four couples; boy in a line on right facing partner in line on left

Counts and Steps:

PART A:

1-16—All four couples advance up the room eight steps; turn, and go back to place eight steps.

1-16—All four couples Gallop up the room eight steps and back eight steps.

PART B:

1-16—First and second couples and third and fourth couples, make Right- and Left-Hand Stars.

1-16—First couple cast; boys left and girls right, others follow. The first couple makes an arch and others Promenade up center.

Repeat the dance.

32. Cotton-Eyed Joe

Description: This is an American Texas style dance with two versions, original and modern.

Music: Rose Valley Music, #PAD 135, or *Cotton-Eyed Joe & Other Texas Dance Hall Favorites Album.*

Formation (original): Double circle, partners facing

Counts and Steps (original): Girls do the opposite.

PART A (ORIGINAL):

1-4—Left heel and toe and step, together, step to the side or CCW; girls use right foot.

5-8—Right heel and toe and step, together, step to the side of CCW; girls use left foot.

1-4—Repeat movements for first set of counts 1-4.

5-8—Repeat movements for first set of counts 5-8.

PART B (ORIGINAL):

1-8—Boys left, CCW four two-steps. Girls right, four two-steps and face.

1-8—Step left foot and close, four times.

1-8—Step right foot and close, four times.

1-8—Face-to-face, then back-to-back; do four two-steps.

Repeat the dance.

Formation (modern): Lines, as if spokes of a wheel, or partners, side-by-side

Counts and Steps (modern):

1-2—Left toes, cross other knee and kick forward.

3-4—One two-step backward, starting on left foot.

5-6—Right toes, cross other knee and kick forward.

7-8—One two-step backward, starting on right foot.

1-8—Repeat the steps in the first set of counts 1 to 8.

1-16—Eight two-steps forward, starting on left foot.

Repeat the dance.

Variation: Another challenge is starting on the right foot and reversing the entire dance.

SUMMARY

This folk dance chapter has shown the cultural diversity of several countries. The method used to introduce these dances is an important aspect of teaching them. You can challenge students to be eager for knowledge of other countries, and this chapter gives enough information to interest the students in learning more about the dances. This chapter can be a resource for the integration of geography and social studies.

SUGGESTED RESOURCES

Resources have been included for all seven chapters with considerable overlap among several chapters. This overlap is due to the large number of resources that have multiple uses for more than one specific content area. They have been arranged in the following categories: professional organizations; records, cassette tapes, CDs, videos, equipment; and books and other written materials. The professional organizations fit into all three categories. At the end of each entry in parentheses are chapter numbers for which the resource appears to be most appropriate. We hope that every need you identify can be solved by these resources.

PROFESSIONAL ORGANIZATIONS

Aerobics & Fitness Association of America, 15250 Ventura Blvd., Ste. 802, Sherman Oaks, CA 91403. (3)

American Alliance for Health, Physical Education, Recreation and Dance, 1900 Association Dr., Reston, VA 22091. (1, 3, 4, 5, 6, & 7)

American College of Sports Medicine, 401 W. Michigan St., Indianapolis 46202-3233. (3)

Country Dance and Song Society, 505 Eighth Ave., New York, 212-594-8833. (1, 4, 5, 6, & 7)

Institute for Aerobic Research, 12330 Preston Rd., Dallas 75230. (3)

International Dance Exercise Association, Idea Foundation, 6190 Cornerstone Court East #202, San Diego 92121. (3)

The Lloyd Shaw Foundation, P.O. Box 134, Sharpes, FL 32959. (1, 2, 3, 4, 5, 6, & 7)

The Sets in Order American Square Dance Society, 462 N. Robertson Blvd., Los Angeles 90048. (4, 5, 6, & 7)

United States Physical Education Association, P.O. Box 5076, Champaign, IL 61825-5076. (1, 2, 3, 4, 5, 6, & 7)

RECORDS, CASSETTE TAPES, CDS, VIDEOS, EQUIPMENT

Callers'-Cuers' Corner, Home of Supreme Audio, 271 Greenway Rd., Ridgewood, NJ 07450, 800-445-7398. (4, 5, 6, & 7)

Dance Record Dist./Folkcraft Records, 10 Fenwick St., Newark, NJ 07114, 201-243-8700. (4, 5, 6, & 7)

Educational Activities, P.O. Box 392, Freeport, NY 11520, 800-645-3739. (4, 5, 6, & 7)

Ken Alan Associates, *Aerobic Beat*, 7985 Santa Monica Blvd., Ste. 109, Los Angeles 90046. (3)

Kimbo Education, P.O. Box 477, 10-16 N. Third Ave., Long Branch, NJ 07740. (4, 5, 6, & 7)

Lebo's of Charlotte, 4118 E. Independence Blvd., Charlotte, NC 28205, 704-535-5000. (3, 4, 5, 6, & 7)

World Wide Games, Box 450, Delaware, OH 43015. (4, 5, 6, & 7)

BOOKS AND OTHER WRITTEN MATERIALS

Callers'-Cuers' Corner, Home of Supreme Audio, 271 Greenway Rd., Ridgewood, NJ 07450, 800-445-7398. (4, 5, 6, & 7)

Casey, B. (1985). *Dance across Texas*. Austin: University of Texas Press. (4, 5, & 7)

Corbin, C.B., & Lindsey, R. (1984). *The ultimate fitness book*. Champaign, IL: Human Kinetics. (3)

Fleming, G.A. (1976). *Creative rhythmic movement: Boys and girls dancing*. Englewood Cliffs, NJ: Prentice Hall. (5 & 6)

Franks, B.D., & Howley, E.T. (1989). *Fitness facts: The healthy living handbook*. Champaign, IL: Human Kinetics. (3)

Human Kinetics Publishers, P.O. Box 5076, Champaign, IL 61820. (1, 2, 3, 4, 5, 6, & 7)

Lane, C. (1995). *Christy Lane's complete book of line dancing*. Champaign, IL: Human Kinetics. (4)

McGreevy-Nichols, S. & Scheff, H. (in press). *Choreography for non-dancers*. Champaign, IL: Human Kinetics. (1, 2, 3)

Purcell, T.M. (1994). *Teaching children dance: Becoming a master teacher*. Champaign, IL: Human Kinetics. (1, 2, 3, 6, 7)

Sachs, C. (1937). *World history of the dance*. New York: W.W. Norton. (7)

Wright, J.P. (1992). *Social dance: Steps to success*. Champaign, IL: Human Kinetics. (2, 3, 4, 5, & 7)

Wright, J.P. (in press). *Teaching social dance: Steps to success*. Champaign, IL: Human Kinetics. (1, 2, 4, 5, & 7)

CREDITS

Acquisitions Editor: Rick Frey, PhD; **Developmental Editor:** Judy Patterson Wright, PhD; **Assistant Editors:** Anna Curry, Dawn Roselund, Myla Smith, and John Wentworth; **Copyeditor:** Denelle Eknes; **Proofreader:** Myla Smith; **Typesetting and Layout:** Ruby Zimmerman; **Text Design:** Stuart Cartwright; **Cover Design:** Jack Davis; **Illustrator:** Mary Yemma Long; **Mac Illustrator:** Denise Lowry; **Photographer (cover):** Ronnie Register; **Interior Photographer:** Ronnie Register; **Models:** Neely Atkinson, Paul Atkinson, Rebecca Bennett, Zack Bennett, Tripp Edwards, Sara Edwards, Thomas Mann, Jr., Cody Mann, Drew Pridgen, Adam Stuver, Christine Stuver, Amanda Wells, and Bridget Wells; **Printer:** Versa Press

ABOUT THE AUTHORS

For more than 25 years John Price Bennett has taught dance to students at every level, from preschool to adult. Both his teaching and work as an administrator at the public school and state levels have given him the opportunity to view hundreds of dance programs and to develop the activities detailed in this book. Since 1992, he has worked as an associate professor in the Department of Health, Physical Education, and Recreation at the University of North Carolina at Wilmington, where most of his efforts are focused on teacher preparation.

John received his master's degree from Virginia Commonwealth University in 1972 and his doctoral degree from Northern Illinois University in 1980. He is in constant demand as a speaker at the international, national, regional, state, and local levels on topics including dance, wellness, K-12 health and physical education programs, and fitness development for all ages. John is a life member of the American Alliance for Health, Physical Education, Recreation and Dance (AAHPERD) and the National Dance Association.

Pamela Coughenour Riemer has been a physical education teacher since 1969. She chairs the physical education department at Sycamore Lane Middle School in Laurinburg, North Carolina. Her tenure there has enabled her to develop and test her ideas about children and dance education in real-life situations.

In 1990 Pam was named the North Carolina Physical Education Teacher of the Year. She also has served on the professional committee for revising the Physical Education Curriculum Standard Course of Study for North Carolina. Her extensive curriculum background has enabled her to help maintain Sycamore Lane Middle School as a North Carolina President's

Council on Physical Fitness Demonstration Center for 7 years. The school also has received the North Carolina Governor's Youth Fitness Award for 3 consecutive years.

Pam received her bachelor's degree in health and physical education from Appalachian State University in 1969 and did graduate work at the University of Oregon in 1972. Pam has made many presentations at the national, regional, state, and local levels on topics related to dance and physical education programs for all age levels. She is the founder and director of the Sycamore Lane Dance Company and a member of AAHPERD and the National Education Association.

More resources for dance, fitness, and movement activities

Theresa M. Purcell, MEd

1994 • Paperback • 136 pp
ISBN 0-87322-479-5
$16.00 ($23.95 Canadian)

(31-minute videotape)

1994 • 1/2" VHS
ISBN 0-87322-704-2
$19.95 ($29.95 Canadian)

Teaching Children Dance offers elementary physical educators a practical approach to teaching developmentally appropriate dance. The book explains the why and how of teaching dance, making it an excellent resource for those who want to teach dance but feel unprepared to do so and for those who are unsure how dance fits into a physical education curriculum. The book also makes an excellent dance methods text for university courses preparing students to become elementary education teachers.

Teaching Children Dance presents 17 practical, child-tested examples of dance activities (called Learning Experiences) that are ideal for grades pre-K through 6. The Learning Experiences are divided into four elements of movement: body awareness, space awareness, effort, and relationships.

The companion *Teaching Children Dance Video* shows three condensed lessons that provide real-world examples of effectively teaching dance to children. The video is geared toward either primary or intermediate levels and includes these lessons: balloon dance, shag dance, and clouds in the sky dance.

Both the video and the book are part of the American Master Teacher Program Content Series. This series is designed to help preservice and in-service teachers gain experience and confidence in teaching the five curriculum areas integral to a complete program: movement concepts and motor skills, games, gymnastics, dance, and fitness.

Special Book and Videotape Package
ISBN 0-87322-705-0
$31.95 ($47.95 Canadian)

The 85 games and activities in this book will help you maximize fitness in your students *and* find activities that they'll enjoy. *Fitness Fun* is a great resource for physical education specialists who teach kindergarten through eighth grade, as well as classroom teachers, program directors, and recreation specialists.

Emily R. Foster, MAT,
Karyn Hartinger, MS, and
Katherine A. Smith, MS

1992 • Paperback • 112 pp
ISBN 0-87322-384-5
$14.95 ($21.95 Canadian)

Rae Pica

Music by Richard Gardzina

1991 • Three-Ring Notebook
5-cassette Set • 152 pp
ISBN 0-87322-301-2
$35.00 ($52.50 Canadian)

Rae Pica

Music by Richard Gardzina

1993 • Three-Ring Notebook
2-cassette Set • 136 pp
ISBN 0-87322-468-X
$29.00 ($43.50 Canadian)

Early Elementary Children Moving & Learning is a complete movement program for 5-to 9-year-olds and a valuable time-saver for teachers. The program includes 40 developmentally appropriate lesson plans with 200 movement activities, plus 5 audiocassettes of original music written specifically for this program!

When it comes to teaching creative movement, active fourth- through sixth-graders can be a tough audience. *Upper Elementary Children Moving & Learning* makes it easy with over 120 problem-solving movement activities within 40 lesson plans, as well as two supplemental music cassettes.

HUMAN KINETICS
The Information Leader in Physical Activity
www.humankinetics.com

2335   **To place an order:** U.S. customers call **TOLL FREE 1-800-747-4457;** customers outside the U.S. use the appropriate address and telephone number shown in the front of this book.

1/00